# THE GREAT TRIBAL WARRIORS of BHARAT

*Praise for the book*

In this, our 75th year of Independence, when PM Shri Narendra Modi has declared the birth anniversary of Bhagwan Birsa Munda as Janjatiya Gaurav Diwas, we needed quality literature around our great tribal freedom fighters. This book is a truly commendable start in that direction.

—**Arjun Munda**, Minister of Tribal Affairs

The establishment narrative tells us that there was only one independence movement in India viz. the non-violent agitation led by Mahatma Gandhi. With complete respect to the greatness of the Mahatma, there is space to include narratives of other movements as well. There was the revolutionary one, led by heroes, such as Bhagat Singh and Netaji Bose. And there was also a tribal one, which has been largely ignored by establishment historians. This wonderful new book by Tuhin Sinha and Ambalika, *The Great Tribal Warriors of Bharat*, sets right this injustice. The independence movement was not just one driven by elite Indian lawyers and businessmen. The life of the independence movement was the common people. A nation that forgets its heroes is doomed. Let us not make that mistake. Let us celebrate the great tribal heroes and heroines who fought the British for the independence of our great nation. Jai Hind!

—**Amish Tripathi**, Author and Director, Nehru Centre, London

The book has some of the finest, yet largely unheard stories of our freedom movement. A must read!

—**Manoj Bajpayee**, Actor

Throughout our history, people from our tribal communities have fought against tyranny and despots! They were also among the first groups to fight the colonizing British, who dealt with them ruthlessly. Their bravery, desire for freedom and preserving their way of life is commendable. This book retells their stories of valour, which are typically ignored by our elitist historians.

—**T.V. Mohandas Pai**, Chairman, Aarin Capital Partners

A rare collection of stories of bravery and sacrifice of some of India's greatest subaltern heroes. The pacy narration and the vivid detailing make these heroes come alive.

—**Aashish Chandorkar**, Public Policy Commentator and Author

# THE GREAT TRIBAL WARRIORS of BHARAT

TUHIN A. SINHA
with AMBALIKA

RUPA

First published by
Rupa Publications India Pvt. Ltd 2022
7/16, Ansari Road, Daryaganj
New Delhi 110002

*Sales Centres:*

Allahabad Bengaluru Chennai
Hyderabad Jaipur Kathmandu
Kolkata Mumbai

Copyright © Tuhin A. Sinha and Ambalika 2022

The views and opinions expressed in this book are the authors' own and the facts are as reported by them which have been verified to the extent possible, and the publishers are not in any way liable for the same.

All rights reserved.
No part of this publication may be reproduced, transmitted, or stored in a retrieval system, in any form or by any means, electronic, mechanical, photocopying, recording or otherwise, without the prior permission of the publisher.

ISBN: 978-93-5520-567-4

Second impression 2022

10 9 8 7 6 5 4 3 2

The moral right of the authors has been asserted.

Printed in India

This book is sold subject to the condition that it shall not, by way of trade or otherwise, be lent, resold, hired out, or otherwise circulated, without the publisher's prior consent, in any form of binding or cover other than that in which it is published.

*This book is for the Adivasis of Bharat.*

*Subjugated and oppressed over the centuries, they need to be at the forefront of the country's resurgence into a Vishwaguru.*

# CONTENTS

*Foreword by Kiren Rijiju* ix
*Introduction* xi

1. Tilka Manjhi (1750–1785) 1
2. Thalakkal Chanthu (1780–1805) 8
3. Budhu Bhagat (1792–1832) 18
4. U Tirot Sing (1800–1833) 26
5. Sidhu, Kanhu, Chand and Bhairab (unknown–1856) 38
6. Baburao Shedmake (1833–1858) and Ramji Gond (1830–1860) 48
7. Tantya Bhil (1842–1889) 58
8. Guru Gobind Giri (1858–1931) 66
9. Jatra Oraon (1894–1916) 77
10. Alluri Sitarama Raju (1897–1924) 84
11. Laxman Nayak (1899–1943) 93
12. Komaram Bheem (1900–1940) 102
13. Helen Lepcha (1902–1980) 109
14. Jaipal Munda (1903–1970) 116
15. Rani Gaidinliu (1915–1993) 125
16. Dashriben Chaudhury (1918–2013) 136
17. Putalimaya Devi (1920–1984) 144

*Acknowledgements* 150
*Bibliography* 153
*Index* 163

# FOREWORD

किरेन रीजीजू
KIREN RIJIJU

मंत्री
विधि एवं न्याय
भारत सरकार
MINISTER
LAW AND JUSTICE
GOVERNMENT OF INDIA

I am delighted to know about Tuhin A. Sinha's new book *The Great Tribal Warriors of Bharat*, co-authored with Ambalika. The book is an eclectic and diverse collection of some of our greatest, though largely unknown, tribal leaders. These leaders, in many ways, led a parallel subaltern freedom movement deep inside our villages and jungles, emaciating the might of the British Empire, which went largely unreported, not just when it was unfolding but also for many decades post Independence.

The credit for bringing these hon'ble tribal revolutionaries to the forefront should rightly go to Hon'ble PM Narendra Modi ji. Hon'ble PM has often invoked the sacrifice of these unsung heroes to galvanize and mainstream our tribal community into the task of nation-building. In a historic move, the birth anniversary of Bhagwan Birsa Munda was declared Janjatiya Gaurav Diwas. In fact, during the entire week starting 15 November, Adivasi icons are commemorated across the country.

The tribal population across the country has been the biggest beneficiary of the social welfare schemes of the government. The PM's Jandhan Yojana, Swachh Bharat Abhiyan, Ude Desh ka Aam Naagrik (UDAN), full electrification of villages, financial inclusion schemes, Har Ghar Nal se Jal Yojana and other schemes have improved the life of our tribal population exponentially. These proactive measures have brought the Northeast closer to Delhi.

I have often felt that the younger generation is not aware of their prodigal ancestry and there is a strong need to pass the stories of tribal heroes on to the succeeding generations. This book celebrates the unsung tribal heroes of our freedom movement by recalling their contributions across the country and in different phases of time. The trajectory of this illustrious journey, from Tilka Manjhi's revolt in 1784 to the profound and nuanced speeches of Jaipal Singh Munda in the Constituent Assembly during 1946–48, in many ways, also marks the evolution of the Adivasi contribution to the country. I'm glad to know that the contribution of Budhu Bhagat and Jatra Oraon, two great tribal leaders from Jharkhand, separated by nearly 100 years, has been covered in the book in detail.

I wish more young minds read this book so that they can enlighten themselves about this forgotten chapter in history. The time has come for the youth to get inspired by the leadership qualities of the great warriors and play a constructive part in the creation of a New India and its emergence as a true *Vishwaguru*.

Kiren Rijiju

# INTRODUCTION

*Movements have narratives. They tell stories, because they are not just about rearranging economics and politics. They also rearrange meaning. And they're not just about redistributing the goods. They're about figuring out what is good.*

—Marshall Ganz, Rita E. Hauser Senior Lecturer in Leadership, Organizing and Civil Society, Kennedy School of Government, Harvard University

This popular quote by Marshall Ganz has an uncanny relevance in the context of India's history, which, in the 75th year of Independence, is increasingly being called out for its selective omissions and commissions. In all our formative years as a nation, we were fed a version of events from our past, which now appears markedly different from what we are rediscovering as we revisit various less-explored chapters of our history.

Various key architects of our nation, be it B.R. Ambedkar, Subhas Chandra Bose or Sardar Vallabhbhai Patel, are finally being studied, based purely on their merit rather than through the hierarchy set by the establishment soon after Independence. Similarly, we are now revisiting our subaltern freedom struggle and its actors, who had always been eclipsed by the stalwarts about whom we grew up reading. Writers and historians are now writing about the subaltern freedom revolutionaries.

They are also revisiting spurious movements, like the Khilafat Movement, and calling out the bluff of an openly Islamist movement being dubbed a freedom struggle.

While growing up in Jamshedpur, Tuhin Sinha was vaguely aware that the areas around the city were, at a point of time, the battlefield of the legendary Birsa Munda. However, barring a slum or a street chowk named after the legend, his story was largely unknown to the world. Today, of course, things have changed. Due to Ranchi's improved air connectivity with the rest of the country, it is highly unlikely for people to not have heard of it since the airport got renamed to the Birsa Munda Airport in 2000. In fact, a top-class international hockey stadium under construction in the neighbouring state of Odisha has recently been named after Birsa Munda and is set to be ready by July 2022.[1] Other states with a large Adivasi population, like Madhya Pradesh,[2] are also invoking the legacy of Birsa Munda with equal alacrity.[3] But back in the '80s, it wasn't the in thing to study or discuss the great Birsa Munda. Instead, our textbooks kept glorifying more elitist leaders. As such, Tuhin had to quench his curiosity about our indigenous freedom struggle with the limited anecdotes that were available through hearsay.

It took us several decades to shed our colonial biases and accord due respect and acknowledgement to our subaltern history. Hon'ble Prime Minister Narendra Modi's personal effort in the ideological transformation of the country is noteworthy. The PM, through his noble *Azadi ka Amrit Mahotsav* initiative, has reignited interest in the unsung heroes of our subaltern

---

[1] 'Birsa Munda International Hockey Stadium ready by July 2022', *Orissa Post*, 19 August 2021, https://bit.ly/3BHxPND. Accessed on 22 February 2022.
[2] 'MP largest Tribal population State', *Daily Pioneer*, 13 November 2021, https://bit.ly/3p6u8w6. Accessed on 22 February 2022.
[3] 'Madhya Pradesh: Martyr Birsa Munda's birth anniversary celebrated with zeal', *The Free Press Journal*, 15 November 2021, https://bit.ly/3BGWCRW. Accessed on 22 February 2022.

tribal freedom movement.[4] Thus, the time is just right to document this movement the way it had been conceived, initiated and carried forward. It predates our mainstream freedom movement, as tribal warriors had been battling the British since the 1780s, if not earlier.

*The Great Tribal Warriors of Bharat* is also important in the modern context, as some of these battles were fought against the forced conversions by missionaries. Predatory conversion is a scourge in several parts of the country even today—particularly in the poorer districts of Jharkhand, Andhra Pradesh, Tamil Nadu, Odisha and Chattisgarh, where it often results in social fissures and tension.[5] This book aims to put these issues in perspective.

It is our humble effort to create a go-to handbook for the contemporary youth. The book has 17 compact chapters, each narrating a previously unheard story from an unknown hinterland, taking the reader on a fascinating journey of how each of these freedom fighters contributed to the larger freedom movement. Each chapter of this book explains the conditions that led to each of the revolts, with specific focus on the psyche of the revolutionary. How each revolt impacted subsequent revolutions also makes for an interesting study.

One of the earliest known tribal freedom fighters was **Baba Tilka Manjhi,** who took up arms against the British in 1784, in what is considered the first major armed rebellion against the colonizers.[6] He mobilized the Santhals to revolt

---

[4]Trivedi, Vivek, '"Azadi Ka Amrit Mahotsav": Shah Says PM to Include Contributions of Unsung Tribal Heroes in History', *News18*, 18 September 2021, https://bit.ly/3p6OGEz. Accessed on 22 February 2022.
[5]'Jharkhand tribal families caned, fined in conversion backlash', *The Times of India*, 2 February 2021, https://bit.ly/36t9rEv. Mukherjee, Krittivas, 'In Jharkhand, Tribes Bear the Cross of Conversion Politics', *Hindustan Times*, 2 December 2014, https://bit.ly/3D85UHs. Accessed on 25 March 2022.
[6]'Tilka Manjhi', Azadi Ka Amrit Mahotsav, Government of India, https://bit.ly/3H6ZGIj. Accessed on 22 February 2022.

against the exploitative, land-grabbing British before he was mercilessly executed for his bravery.

The next important tribal warrior covered in the book is **Thalakkal Chanthu** of Wayanad in Kerala. An archer and commander-in-chief of the Kurichiyan soldiers of the Pazhassi Raja, he fought the British forces in the Wayanad jungles during the first decade of the nineteenth century.

The Kurichiyan revolt was followed by an uprising in the Khasi Hills in the Northeast and the Kol revolt in Jharkhand, both occurring in the early 1830s. Present-day Meghalaya and Jharkhand's Ranchi region witnessed massive revolts led by **U Tirot Sing** and **Budhu Bhagat**, respectively.

These revolutionaries were followed by several tribal freedom fighters whose revolts across the nation were a precursor to the 1857 war of independence. This includes the Murmu brothers **Sidhu** and **Kanhu**, the key architects of the Santhal insurrection of 1855, which originated in Sahibganj district in present-day Jharkhand, and **Baburao Shedmake**, a Gond tribal warrior who ignited a revolt in Maharashtra.

Equally interesting is how **Tantya Bhil**, the revolutionary from Madhya Pradesh, fought against British rule for over a decade with bravery and passion.

The early decades of the twentieth century saw similar tribal uprisings across the country. Some of the key revolutionaries during this period were **Rani Gaidinliu** from Manipur, **Jatra Oraon** from Ranchi, **Helen Lepcha** from Sikkim, **Putalimaya Devi Tamang** from Kurseong, **Alluri Sitarama Raju** from Andhra Pradesh, **Laxman Nayak** from Odisha, among others. Equally inspiring is the story of **Dashriben Chaudhury**, a tribal woman born in 1918 in Vedchhi village in the Tapi district of Gujarat, who turned into a satyagrahi after meeting with Mahatma Gandhi at a very young age. Another story worth narrating is that of **Jaipal Munda**, India's former hockey captain, who represented the Adivasi community in the Constituent

Assembly under Dr B.R. Ambedkar. The border areas of present-day Gujarat and Rajasthan talk about **Guru Gobind Giri**, who was a social and religious reformer and fought for the rights of the Bhil tribals. His contribution was well-regarded among the tribes. He is also credited with starting the Bhagat Movement.

This was followed by a small uprising led by a Gond tribal warrior **Komaram Bheem** in Asifabad, a town near the present-day Adilabad district of Telangana. **Birsa Munda**, the most iconic of these freedom fighters, is not a part of this collection, as Tuhin has recently published a separate book on him.[7]

It may be noted that all of these tribal icons have been consciously referred to as revolutionaries, irrespective of whether they employed violent means. They are revolutionaries because they inspired change and leadership among the downtrodden Adivasis and assiduously aspired to give their communities a better life!

In a humble attempt to honour these unsung heroes, this book cover acts as a wall of fame, where their names are etched in dust and grime, commemorating their fight for Bharat Mata. The list, though small, is an apt microcosm of the gigantic movement that was pivotal to our quest for political freedom.

---

[7]Sinha, Tuhin, *The Legend of Birsa Munda*, Manjul Pub., New Delhi, 2021, 400.

# 1
# TILKA MANJHI
(1750–1785)

## The Robinhood of Jungle Terry

In the winter of 1783, 29-year-old Augustus Cleveland, the collector of Bhagalpur, was preparing to lead a force of armed sepoys to quell some disturbance that had erupted in the area. From what he had gathered, this was just a case of a group of hill men expressing their displeasure, albeit in an exaggerated manner, over some petty issue. Cleveland would have preferred the mode of conciliation, though. This was his style of administration, and where his talent lay as an efficient civil servant of the Bengal Civil Service. He had brought about several positive changes and his bosses in Calcutta were in awe of the results he had produced. The revolting hill men, however, had a different point of view. So, Cleveland rode out of Tilha Kothi, a large building of Italian design situated atop a hill by the Ganges, battle-ready and armed with intelligence of the guerrilla warfare that awaited him, fully confident of conquest.

Riding out at full charge, he passed by a dense clump of trees that momentarily caused him to slow down. As he worked to find his way ahead, he felt a piercing pain seize him. He looked down and saw an arrow protruding from his chest. It was one of the poison-loaded arrows used by the hill men during war. He realized at once that only one of the hill men would have had the courage to do this—the Santhal chief with bloodshot eyes, Tilka Manjhi, who, thus, unwittingly became the first Adivasi leader from the Santhal community to take up arms against the British.

## A divine right to rule

Tilka and the Santhals were used to equality and justice through self-governance. They considered the dominating presence of the white men—the *dikus*[1]—unwarranted and wanted them evicted. Cleveland, on the other hand, considered himself a just dispenser of the law. He wanted the Santhals to comply with the British administration. The problems created by this scenario had no resolution in sight. This wasn't the kind of fiasco Cleveland had anticipated in his already successful career. Neither was this the kind of fate that Tilka had envisioned for his people when he had taken over the reins of chiefdom from his father, a divine honour reserved only for the 12 totemic clans among the Santhals.

Born on 11 February 1750, Sundara Murmu's (also known as Chundra) heir grew up much like the youth of his age while also preparing for his future as the manjhi—the chief of the clan. Every Santhal hamlet has a *manjhi hanan*, who is considered the father of the community. The *manjhi hanan* receives divine powers through prayers and passes them on to a subsequent descendant, who is referred to as the manjhi.

Santhal tradition requires the manjhi to become adept at archery and wrestling—skills that would prove his physical prowess as the chief. As for the wisdom to maintain peace and prosperity in the community, it is bestowed by the *Marang Buru*, the Santhal supreme deity, at their sacred grove, when

---

[1] Diku is the Santhal word for outsiders. In this case, it refers to the British East India Company officials.

the time is right. While being groomed to be the manjhi, the young Tilka acted as the *jog-manjhi*, the chief of all the children of the hamlet, akin to a crown prince.

Around the same time, halfway across the globe, a young British man, Augustus Cleveland had applied to the East India Company to be deployed as a civil servant. He was born into a wealthy and distinguished family that had served the Royal Navy Admiralty for many generations. After graduating in writing, arithmetic and mercantile accounts, the 17-year-old Augustus arrived in India as a writer for the Company in 1771.

## Taxation and famine

In 1765, Robert Clive had signed the Treaty of Allahabad with Mughal Emperor Shah Alam II and secured the right to collect revenue from Bengal, Bihar, Orissa and present-day Jharkhand. He had little inkling of what to expect from the province he was sent to tax, except to generate huge profits for the Company. Much of these newly acquired territories came under Jungle Terry or Jungle Terai—the forested lowlands that lay to the west of present-day Bhagalpur and covered large parts of West Bengal, Bihar and Jharkhand. It included Rajmahal Hills in present-day Jharkhand, surrounded by Kharagpur, Munger, Birbhum and Jamui. Rich in timber, tasar silk, coal and iron ore, this was a tract of land that had never been subjugated, even during the time of Akbar. The people here had never owed allegiance to either the Mughals or the nawabs of Bengal. They were self-governed and sustained the economy on their own terms through cultivation and hunting. Taxation was an alien concept to them. So, to find their property confiscated upon failing to pay taxes was beyond their comprehension.

As the village headman, getting the British administration to revoke the taxation policy became Tilka's first challenge. This issue was yet unaddressed, when the next misfortune struck—

the crops failed in 1768 due to a failure of the monsoon. The situation was aggravated further, and, by 1770, famine had set in. Tilka led his kinsmen out of Jungle Terry in search of food and hope for a life without the burden of tax. But such a place could not be found. What irked Tilka was that, even in such a situation, the British government was more concerned about their revenue collection target not being met. While the Company officials calculated a revised, higher tax rate, Tilka and his fellow manjhis saw their people die of hunger and sell their cattle, seeds, tools, implements and even children, to pay their taxes. Those who survived ate leaves and grass, while the government sold whatever grains were procured at high rates elsewhere. Later that year, the rains did come. But instead of providing relief, the monsoon unleashed an epidemic of smallpox. In 1771, the province was a dismal picture of barren lands and a glaring absence of people.

Augustus started his career under these circumstances. His influential connections—most notably the one with Sir John Shore (later Baron John Teignmouth)—ensured that he was rapidly promoted to the assistant collectorship of Bhagalpur and Rajmahal Hills in 1776, eventually becoming the collector of the region in 1779.[2] Unlike Augustus, Tilka's lineage of mystical origins was rooted in steep morals, which meant having to constantly fight for justice.

## Conciliation vs guerrilla action

The lack of any initiative by the government to improve the economic condition of the people infuriated Tilka. In 1778, he issued the call to end *diku raj*. He acted swiftly, creating the Mukti Dal, a group of youngsters trained by Tilka that successfully

---

[2]Marshall, P. J. 'Suresh Chandra Ghosh: The Social Condition of the British Community in Bengal', *Bulletin of the School of Oriental and African Studies*, Vol. 35, No. 1, 1972, pp. 172–173, doi:10.1017/S0041977X00107724.

drove out the Company's army from the Ramgarh camp near Bhagalpur. Tilka led from the front, looting the government treasury and giving away the money to the needy. The masses followed suit by unleashing a host of disruptive activities like looting the dak services and residences of government officials. This event marked the onset of guerrilla warfare that would last for long.

While people focused on pushing out the Company rule, the government busied itself with the zamindars—they were encouraged to lure villagers into tilling their lands. This led to a group of Santhals migrating to the Rajmahal Hills, where the Paharias lived. The Paharias were a race of hill tribes who hunted and plundered. All attempts by the British to turn them into settled cultivators had failed, due to which the fertile lands of the hills lay barren. To the British, this amounted to the loss of revenue. The arrival of the Santhals was, thus, a boon to the government.

However, the Santhals soon discovered that through a policy of conciliation laid down by Captains Browne and Brooke between 1772 and 1779, the British had converted Rajmahal Hills into a safe haven for the Paharias called the Damin-i-Koh. As the collector, Cleveland intensified these efforts, which included providing lifelong pensions and rent-free land to the Paharia chiefs, establishing Hill Assemblies and bazaars for bartering their goods, raising a corps of hill archers and even building a school for the children.

To Tilka, it seemed as if Cleveland was using a two-pronged approach of subjugation of the Santhals and conciliation towards the Paharias at the same time. He vehemently opposed this and, from 1780 onwards, he embarked on a quest to ensure that either the Santhals received the same conciliatory treatment as the Paharias or Cleveland and his system were evicted. Openly at war against the British now, Tilka and the Santhals lost no opportunity to attack Cleveland.

## Death and legacy

Tilka Manjhi's attack on Cleveland on a winter morning of 1783 left the latter bedridden for three months, after which he was advised to proceed to the Cape of Good Hope for recuperation. In early January 1784, he boarded the *Atlas Indiaman* in the company of Marian Hastings—the wife of Warren Hastings.[3] However, by the time the vessel reached the mouth of the Hooghly, he had died. His body was put in a barrel of spirits and brought back to be buried in the South Park Street cemetery in Calcutta. A huge monument was erected by the Court of Directors of the East India Company in honour and recognition of his service.

Given Cleveland's proximity to the powers that were at Fort William, the attack on him was regarded as an attack on the authorities. Already harsh with their economic policies, the British authorities became even more brutal with the desire to avenge Cleveland's death. A massive manhunt was launched for Tilka, and he was to be brought in dead or alive.

It took the Company army another year to track and nab the Santhal chief. After trying every trick in the book to isolate him in the mountainous tracks and offering a few villagers luxurious items that tempted them to give away Tilka's whereabouts, he was finally caught on 12 January 1785. Upon capture, the British soldiers tied Tilka to four horses and dragged him all the way to the collector's residence at Bhagalpur. His body was soaked in blood, yet he was alive. The next day, he was publicly hanged from a banyan tree. Today, the site is the residence of the superintendent of police of Bhagalpur. On the contrary, the Tilha Kothi went on to be a temporary residence to Rabindranath Tagore, where he is believed to have written

---

[3] '1996 | Live auction 5600 | Anglo-Indian', Christie's, https://bit.ly/3M3jOxN. Accessed on 14 April 2022.

a portion of his Nobel Prize-winning work, *Gitanjali*.[4] Today, it houses the Department of Ancient Indian History, Culture and Archaeology of the Tilka Manjhi Bhagalpur University.

However, written records have a different story to tell. While Cleveland remained fresh in the minds of the Paharias as 'Chilmil Saheb' 160 years after his death, in stark contrast, as Sir John Houlton ICS found out, there were no references to Tilka Manjhi. In fact, the records even state that the cause for Cleveland's death was his poor health due to the harsh climatic conditions as well as the stress of being a civil servant. Consequently, history tends to question if Tilka Manjhi was a myth or a reality. In truth, Tilka Manjhi's uprising was no flash in the pan. It partially kept in check the exploitative and avariciously expanding British Empire that had, until then, been unresisted in reaching newer far-flung territories. Thus, Tilka Manjhi had, in his own way, set the stage for the many revolts yet to spring in the region, most notable of which were the Munda uprising and the Santhal *hul*.[5]

---

[4]Sinha, Raman, 'Tilha Kothi – Bhagalpur's Historic Address', *Live History India*, 19 July 2018, https://bit.ly/3K1gnHd. Accessed on 22 February 2022.
[5]*Hul* is the Santhal word for revolution/insurrection.

# 2

## THALAKKAL CHANTHU

(1780–1805)

### In Pursuit of Pepper and Paddy

Nestled between the Malabar plains, Nilgiri Hills, the Mysore plateau and the ghats of Coorg is Wayanad. Originally a forest country, it was ruled by the Vedars or hunter kings, until they were conquered by the kings of Kottayam and Kurumbranad. The conquering rajas had first partitioned the region between themselves but, eventually, all of Wayanad came under the rule of the Kottayam kings, with Mananthavady becoming its capital. To assist in this war, the Kottayam raja had brought with him a set of hill people adept at archery. They may have belonged to the nearby Kurichi hill country or been related distantly to a class of Nayars from the Travancore region. But based on their archery skills, the king found it fit to call them 'Kurichiyan', derived from *'kurivechavan'* or 'he who took aim'. After the Vedar wars, the Kurichiyans settled in Wayanad, the western branch of the Kottayam dynasty, practising agriculture or serving as archers in the army of the Kottayam king, Kerala Varma Pazhassi Raja.

Kerala Varma greatly admired the Kurichiyans. It is said that he used to openly declare that as long as they were with him, he needed no one else during a war. The simple-minded and honest Kurichiyans reciprocated Kerala Varma's sentiments with their fierce loyalty towards him. They would go to any extent to honour and protect their King.

Thalakkal Chanthu was the chief archer of this unit. Born into the Karkottil family that lived in the tiny village of Kunhome in the present-day Thondernad panchayat, about 24 kilometres away from Mananthavady, Chanthu grew up to be a skilled archer.[1] He was as swift with the bow and arrow as with his mind skills. This made him utterly indispensable to Edachena Kunkan—the commander of the army. Under Kunkan, a superior warrior himself, Chanthu further sharpened his capacity to design strategic military plans, especially under impossible situations. Kunkan soon came to regard Chanthu, believed to be in his early twenties around the time, as his right-hand man.

## The siege

During the second Anglo-Mysore war of the 1780s, when Hyder Ali laid siege to Tellicherry, Kerala Varma supplied an army of 2,000 Kurichiyans to Robert Taylor, the chief of the English settlement at Tellicherry. The siege was broken successfully and much of the credit for this went to the Kunkan–Chanthu duo for their fearless and intelligent battle plans. Robert Taylor assured Kerala Varma protection in return for his assistance in their continuing war with Mysore, which Tipu Sultan was ruling. Although Wayanad had remained unaffected by the incessant invasions of the Mysore sultans so far, Kerala Varma was happy to have the friendship of the British and be considered their ally. However, this friendship was short-lived. With the fall of Tipu Sultan, through the Treaty of Seringapatam in 1792, Malabar was ceded to the East India Company and Wayanad

---

[1]This information has been sourced from the Thalakkal Chanthu Memorial in Wayanad.

was annexed, which was a shock for Kerala Varma. With the annexation, the friendship between the Pazhassi Raja and the British died a premature death.

The annexation also set the stage for the Company to begin signing treaties with kings to demand the payment of protection tribute[2] in the form of natural produce alone. With this, the East India Company further strengthened its monopoly over pepper, the black gold of Malabar. Tax collection was at the core of these new one-year treaties that started from October 1792. The Raja was required to hand over at least 500 *kantis*[3] of pepper produced from Kottayam as well as pay a sum of 20,000 rupees in two instalments per year in arrears. In the spring of 1793, this was hiked to 55,000 rupees and at least 700–800 *kantis* of pepper.

Matters took a turn for the worse when Vira Varma, the king of Kurumbranad and the arch rival of Kerala Varma, was appointed as the tax collector for Wayanad. The ever-seeking-to-please Vira Varma, who signed a treaty with the British with the sole intention of personal gain—both material and political—took up the role assigned to him with great enthusiasm. He was also in the habit of sending daily reports of all events that occurred in Kottayam to the East India Company officials, a factor that was instrumental in crushing any opposition from the natives. For the British, Vira Varma was the perfect person to keep supplying them with a lot of information that would ultimately help them completely take over Malabar. Eventually, Vira Varma usurped the seat of power and evicted Kerala Varma from the scene. Deprived of his palace, troops and treasury, Kerala Varma was forced to retire to the interiors of the forests.

---

[2] A payment in money or other valuables made by one ruler or nation to another in acknowledgment of submission or as the price of protection or security.

[3] A unit of measurement, commonly known as candy, ranging between 560 lbs and 640 lbs.

## An action-packed exile

As the exiled King moved into his new settlement, he was much surprised, delighted and relieved to be joined by thousands of Kurichiyans, his subjects, led by his commander-in-chief, Thalakkal Chanthu. One of the many things that the Kurichiyans immediately started doing was gathering intelligence about the activities of Vira Varma and the Company. This was critical for two reasons—first, to stay informed about the welfare of his remaining subjects and second, to keep a tab on Vira Varma.

Even as this new set of fighters was getting ready for battle, Kerala Varma defied the Company's treaty by destroying the pepper plants so that they could not collect any tax and hoped for a meaningful dialogue with the Company officials. It was only in December 1793 that the East India Company agreed to make tax exemptions for temples, donate one-fifth of the taxes towards their upkeep and another one-fifth to support Kerala Varma, in recognition of his support during the Anglo-Mysore wars.

Vira Varma, in the meantime, unleashed his own campaign of taxing Kottayam by four times the expected amount. Unable to meet such demands, there was a mass exodus of farmers, which, in turn, led to poor levels of pepper production.

In protest, Kerala Varma, now accompanied by the newly trained Kurichiyan army, did not allow any British officials to collect tax till 1799 by periodically disrupting things. In 1802, the Company issued a new tax assessment which increased individual tax by 20 per cent in gold *fanams*[4] and 10 per cent in silver *fanams*; the government's share in rice production was raised to 40 per cent and the yield for a coconut palm was put

---

[4]The *fanam* was a form of currency in the Madras Presidency that was in use until 1815. It was used alongside the Indian rupee, also issued by the Presidency. A rupee was equivalent to 12 *fanams*.

at an unrealistic 48 nuts. To meet these demands, people started selling their properties.

One day, a peon of native origin, working for the East India Company, came knocking at the hut of a Kurichiyan. He was on duty to collect the paddy tax. Chanthu happened to be present at the scene since he had been out spying on Vira Verma. He found the peon's demand totally unacceptable. So, he promptly reported the matter to Edechena Kunkan. Kunkan responded to the peon's demand by killing him. This incident forewarned all parties involved of how nasty the situation could get in the future. As if in response to this incident, Chanthu and Kunkan began to plan a large-scale retaliation.

## Attack on the garrison

On the morning of 11 October 1802, Chanthu led a band of 400–500 bow-and-arrow-wielding Kurichiyans to the Panamaramkottah (palmyra tree fort) garrison that was being held by a detachment of 70 men of the 1st battalion of the 4th Bombay Native Infantry under Captain J.P. Dickenson and Lieutenant A. Maxwell.[5] Breaking themselves up into three parties, they attacked the barracks, the officers' homes and the sepoys, simultaneously. The cantonment and kutchery (the British magistrate's court) were burnt. They secured all the arms, blew up the ammunition that had been stocked at Captain Dickenson's house and massacred the entire detachment. Only one servant of Captain Dickenson escaped. This was a major victory for Kerala Varma but a shock for the Company that had come to believe that the exiled King would not cause any further trouble.

While Chanthu's skilful execution of eliminating the

---

[5]William, Logan, 'Malabar Manual, Vol. 1', Internet Archive, https://bit.ly/3vWfiuE. Accessed on 02 May 2022.

garrison won him accolades from the King and Kunkan, the episode understandably infuriated Colonel Arthur Wellesley, the governor of Mysore, who was also in charge of the military control of Malabar. The future Duke of Wellington, Arthur Wellesley had no fondness for Wayanad, which he described as a jungle country and the native people as, 'savage and cruel.'[6] Furthermore, the complicated geography of Wayanad, which suited Chanthu and the Kurichiyans' guerrilla warfare, added to Wellesley's military difficulties, as it made troop movement challenging. What made him even more livid was that a few miles west of Panamaram, at Pulinjal, were the headquarters of the battalion where Major Drummond, thoroughly shaken by this act, sat quietly in his cantonment, taking no action. Wellesley dispatched reinforcements and expressed his displeasure with the Major's actions, asserting that he needed to get over his supineness and suppress the rebellion with the forces being sent for assistance, rather than keeping them shut in the fort or cantonment.[7]

## Call to arms

Meanwhile, encouraged by the success at Panamaramkottah, Chanthu reached the Pulpally Pagoda—an old temple which had become a meeting place for the Kurichiyans—and issued a call for the natives to join him. Such was the dynamism of his personality and so deep was the reverence of the people for Kerala Varma that 3,000 men assembled in no time. With such strong backing, Chanthu stepped up his attacks on the British. In the latter half of 1802, he blocked a column of the

---

[6]'Wayanad and its brush with a former British PM and Battle of Waterloo hero', *The Economic Times*, 21 April 2019, https://bit.ly/3vStCGk. Accessed on 9 March 2022.
[7]Wellesley, Arthur, *Supplementary Despatches and Memoranda of Field Marshal Arthur Duke of Wellington, K.G.*, John Murray, London, 1859.

British army on the way to Mananthavady and, in 1803, attacked an output at Pazhassi. Guerrilla warfare continued for the next year. It was simply impossible for the government to defeat the Chanthu-led Kurichiyans who clearly had an upper hand in the fight despite not possessing modern weaponry. Failing to do anything noteworthy, Principal Collector of Malabar Thomas Warden announced a reward of 1,000 *pagodas*[8] (₹10,000) for any help in arresting Chanthu. But the reward remained unclaimed.

The dashed hopes of winning against the Kurichiyans finally began to be salvaged when, by the end of 1804, Lieutenant Colonel A. Macleod was appointed to command the troops in Malabar and Canara. He was invested with special powers to impose martial law on anyone found possessing arms. At the same time, Thomas H. Baber was appointed as the sub-collector of Malabar in the revenue department. Baber was a stubborn administrator when it came to achieving the tasks assigned to him. True to his reputation, he got to work at once, suppressing the disturbances caused by the Kurichiyans.

Baber figured out that apart from the primitive yet powerful weapons, it was the ability to be slippery like an eel that was giving Chanthu and his aides an upper hand. He was quick to enforce the order imposed by the former Principal Collector Major William Macleod that made the possession of any arms illegal. Only government employees could own them. Those found violating this were tried under martial law and were instantly gunned down or sent to the public gallows. This came as a big setback for the Kurichiyans across Wayanad for they used their bows and arrows not just to fight in war but also to hunt. Their weapons were sacred to them and they kept them at special altars erected in their houses. Now, they had to part with them. Simultaneously, Baber widened and strengthened

---

[8] A *pagoda* was a type of currency minted by Indian dynasties and colonial rulers.

his network of informers. He rewarded them handsomely both in cash and kind when they brought news that benefitted him. Essentially, Baber was trying to rebuild Panamaramkottah and eliminate the 'insurgents', while being open to offering pardon. By May 1805, Lieutenant Colonel A. Macleod returned to Cannanore after handing over the charge of the conflicted regions to Captains Innes, Watson and Clapham, who would continue the intense combing operation.

**The end and its aftermath**

With these new developments, Chanthu, Kunkan and Kerala Varma realized that, one way or the other, the end was near. However, they did not give up and never considered surrendering. This meant that they had to be constantly on the move and could certainly not travel together. On 15 November 1805, as Chanthu was on his way to meet Kunkan, he was intercepted by one of Baber's informers. Swiftly acting on this piece of news, Baber captured Chanthu and had him publicly executed by hanging him under a koli tree, which still stands today. When the news of Chanthu's martyrdom reached Kerala Varma and Kunkan, both were overcome with grief as well as vengeance.

Later that month, on 30 November, during a forest patrol by the 1st battalion of the 4th regiment under Captain Clapham, along with a hundred armed peons from Baber's kutchery, under Baber's direction, came face to face with Kerala Varma, Kunkan and a hundred of their soldiers on the banks of Mavila Thod, a stream. Baber ordered the force to advance. At this point, Charen Subedar from Captain Watson's force and Karunakara Menon, the head clerk of the kutchery, rushed forward to attack the Raja and his party.

Luckily for Menon, the Raja's gun failed to fire. However, Kunkan started shooting and was killed in the crossfire. Menon later on went on to claim in writing that it was he who pulled the fatal shot at the Raja during the short but intense fight.[9] However, Baber credits the act to both Menon and Charan Subedar. At the end of the fight, Baber arranged for the mortal remains of the Raja to be carried in his own palanquin back to Mananthavady, where he was cremated by the bank of the Kabini River with full royal honours because it is believed that Baber and the government had a high regard for the Raja. The cremation spot has been preserved to this day.

Kunkan's nephew, Emman, and his younger brother, Komappen, who participated in the rebellion, were arrested, court martialled at Seringapatam and tried on 31 March 1809. They pleaded not guilty but were sentenced to death by hanging. However, there are records of an appeal.[10] So, it is possible that the sentence was commuted to exile to the Prince of Wales Island.

## Committing sedition

The government also declared that by fighting against them, the natives had committed sedition. Hence, none of their families could own property. They were even denied land for cremation and their family members could not get jobs. Three generations since then, Kunkan's family still lives on in Wayanad with no change in their circumstances.

As for other Kurichiyans and tribe members who had supported the insurrection, their properties were confiscated

---

[9] 'The Slayer of Pazhassi Raja', Hamlet in Monsoon Blog of Ramachandran # History,Life and Polemics, https://bit.ly/3s06iDI. Accessed on 15 April 2022; 'Thomas Baber's account of the death of the Pazhassi Rajah, Part 4', Malabar Days, https://bit.ly/3jC97pY. Accessed on 15 April 2022.

[10] 'Edachena Kunkan and the Siege of Panamaram Fort', Hamlet in Monsoon Blog of Ramachandran # History, Life and Polemics, https://bit.ly/3OUNdN9. Accessed on 03 May 2022.

along with their right to agriculture by clearing forests. Tax arrears were building up exponentially and to collect these in cash only, the officials had resorted to intolerable cruelty. The Kurichiyans, bereft of anything to even subsist on, were forced to become slaves. It was against this backdrop that the next Kurichiyan revolt broke out on 25 March 1812, around the time of the mutiny at Quilon. In many ways, it was the revolt of 1805 repeating itself—this time with the nephew of the martyred Kerala Varma. Rama Nambi, the Kurichiyan leader, crippled the forces of Colonel James Tagg, who was taken by complete surprise. '*Watta toppikare natil ninnum purathakanam*', broadly translating to, 'Throw out of the country, the round cap-wearers', was the battle cry that rent the air. Once more, relief troops had to be summoned, this time from Mysore, Seringapatam and Cannanore.

Unleashing extreme terror, the British troops eventually subjugated the uprising and quiet was restored. This rebellion lasted less than two months but was a success because it finally highlighted the necessity to do away with the extortionate revenue policy of the East India Company.

# 3

## BUDHU BHAGAT

(1792–1832)

### The Rock that Shrieked for Freedom

When Emperor Shah Alam II handed over the diwani of Bengal, Bihar and Orissa to the British in 1765, it included the Chota Nagpur plateau and its nearby regions. The British started their campaign of force-fitting their administrative system over the existing one in the region by indirectly ruling it through the local rajas. Ever since, these regions, including Ramgarh, became a hotbed of unrest. However, this unrest was eventually subdued, and in the early 1830s, the region was rather peaceful. This peace did not last long. Trouble first broke out in the Khunti district of Jharkhand. On 11 December 1831, a group of Kol[1] tribesmen from the villages of Kochang and Jamro (erstwhile Jamoor), in the present-day Khunti and West Singhbhum districts, respectively, raided another village in Khunti called Komang (earlier, Kumang). They escaped with a herd of 200 cattle that belonged to a well-known farmer. While such instances

---

[1] During the British times, the term 'Kol' included the Santhal, Oraon, Munda and Ho tribes. Post Independence, the usage of the term has been restricted to refer to the tribes that speak the Mundari language.

were not unheard of, this incidence was followed by a second attack by 700 men on four other villages of Sonepur Pargana on 20 December 1831. As part of this attack, the men burned, plundered and killed two men.[2] This got then Magistrate-Judge Seignilay Thomas Cuthbert worried. With the December 1831 attacks, everything seemed unsettled.

## From a handful of earth to a document

One factor common to both these attacks was that outsiders had been targeted. The victims had been non-tribals, mostly Muslims and Sikhs, who owned several villages. The lack of hospitality and respect that the Kols felt for the non-tribals wasn't a new development. It had started brewing back when the local rajas, initially belonging to one of the many tribes, had Hinduized themselves by beginning to follow Hindu rituals and regularly intermarrying with neighbouring Hindu families, to be at par with the ruling Rajputs and Kshatriyas elsewhere. They had also brought in other Hindus and Muslims who were either moneylenders or merchants into the fold. The rajas allotted land and villages to the diwans, who ran the courts, moneylenders and merchants in recognition of their services. This is how a new system of land ownership and revenue collection was introduced to the Kol society. Until then, land was given by the village priest and headman to a person by showing it to them in the presence of a witness and picking up a piece of earth as a sign of acceptance. They did not need the paraphernalia of formal documents or pattas. The Kols found the new system violating their goodwill and trust-based style of conducting their lives and livelihood.

The arrival of the British made matters worse. Not only

---

[2] 'Kol Resurrection of Chota-nagpur', Internet Archive, https://bit.ly/3uuNKf3. Accessed on 25 March 2022.

did they fail to get the local rajas to be compliant to their administrative ways, they also embarked on a spree of taxation with no understanding of the local tribal sentiments. As a result, most of their early time and resources were spent dealing with corruption and solving feuds within and between the royal families. With the introduction of house tax, tax on *hanria* (rice beer) and the introduction of poppy cultivation, the tribal folk started resenting Cuthbert.

### Battles with the Company

Needless to say, the December 1831 attacks captured the imagination of the Kols. Primarily a hardworking, patient, truthful and resilient race, the Kols shed all inhibitions when it came to defending their pride—their land. The 'arrow of war'[3] was passed from village to village as an invitation to join the call of rising against the 'outsiders'. A village that chose to join returned the arrow intact, while the ones that didn't returned it broken in half. This was the start of the rebellion and, in its initial stages, was led collectively by the *munda* (village headman) and *manki* (circle headman) of the particular pargana. Cuthbert's men, consisting of a head constable, two barkandazes[4] and 30 armed men paled in strength against close to a thousand Kols. Only 14 of Cuthbert's men survived when they went out to rein in the troublemakers.

The attacks continued through Christmas day into January 1832, in rapid succession. With every episode, the Kols became more gruesome. The Ho sub clan of the Kols was referred to as 'Larka' Kols by their adversaries, particularly the British, due

---

[3] A practice prevalent among the Kols to pass an arrow from village to village as a summons for arms when preparing for war.

[4] The barkandazes were disbanded soldiers of the Muslim armies or zamindars who either plundered for a living or offered their soldiering services to anyone in return for money and other riches.

to their ability to fight and create disturbances.[5]

By the time reinforcements, led by Captain Thomas Wilkinson, the acting political agent to the Governor General of India, arrived from Ramgarh on 14 January 1832, the rebellion had taken over all of Chota Nagpur. Nevertheless, the Ramgarh Battalion did its best to ward off some 3,000 Kols, amid supply shortages and a lack of men, as the Kols advanced to the nearby dependent parganas of Tamar, Bundu, Baranda, Silli, Rahi, Barwa and Tori. The kings of all these parganas fled to Palamu or Jungle Mahal with their families, knowing fully that, if caught, they would be mercilessly killed. While the palaces of the kings were spared, all the houses in the villages were razed to the ground.

By end of January, the Ramgarh Battalion was strengthened by the arrival of cavalry and native infantry from Danapur, Banaras and Barrackpore under the command of Major Sutherland and Captain H.R. Impey. The East India Company troops were now convinced that the Kol's bow, battleaxe and arrow stood no chance against their pistols and musketry.

## Facing the 'Rock'

In Silli (Silligaon), present-day Silagain village in the Chanho block in Ranchi, Jharkhand, Budhu Bhagat held guard against the Company troops. An aged, experienced and revered figure among the Larka Kols, Budhu was also a *bhumij*.[6] So, Budhu was naturally inclined to revolt against the changes ushered in by the British, standing like a 'rock' between the alien changes and the existing traditional system. Together with his sons, nephews,

---

[5]Nath, Sanjay, 'Remembering Poto Ho: The Leader of Adivasi Anti-British Resistance in Kolhan (1836-37)', *Journal of Adivasi and Indigenous Studies*, Vol. 9, No. 1, 2019, pp. 1-25.
[6]This means the one who is born from the soil—the original owner or cultivator of the land.

brothers and other relatives, he presented a solid, impenetrable human frontier. The modern weapons of the British failed before the guerrilla warfare and agility of the Kols, led by Budhu, which triggered a deadlock. Keen to quickly end the unrest, the joint commissioners for Chota Nagpur announced a reward of 1,000 rupees for those who could capture Budhu. Until then, the British forces had neither been able to kill nor capture a single *munda* or *manki*. By capturing or killing Budhu, they hoped to send out a strong message to the Kols that they should end the insurrection.

On 14 February 1832, a little after daybreak, Captain Impey arrived at Silli with four companies of the 50th Bengal Native Infantry and 40 troopers. By his account, this march was carried out in 'greatest secrecy'.[7] It was widely suspected that Bhola Singh, a part-time farmer and notorious dacoit who had recently been released from the Sherghati jail, had a role to play in the eventual fall of Budhu. Bhola was not on good terms with Budhu and had even unsuccessfully attempted to burn down Silligaon once. In response, Budhu had successfully burnt down Bhola's village. Due to frequent highway robberies, Bhola was in the bad books of the British as well. So, when war broke out between the Kols and the British, he saw it as an opportunity to win favour with the British by siding with them, and settle his score with Budhu.

By the daybreak of 14 February, the British reached Silli and launched their attack on a village that was just waking up to their usual morning chores. This came as a surprise to the Kols, who had, only a few days ago, seen a British military officer wave his hat at them in a friendly way. So, at first, unable to understand what was happening, they retreated to

---

[7]Jha, J.C., 'A Sad Episode of the Kol Insurrection (1832)', *Proceedings of the Indian History* Congress, Vol. 42, 1981, pp. 413–418, https://bit.ly/3JERaCn. Accessed on 24 March 2022.

the hills. This bought them time to assume positions across the hills from where they could shower their arrows on the invading cavalry. An intense hand-to-hand battle ensued with swords and axes. Sadly for the Kols, they were losing. Around 150 Kols were killed in the encounter. This included Budhu, seven of his sons and his brother. Since Captain Impey was not able to identify Budhu, the heads of three Kol males were cut off and carried away for identification. The decapitated bodies were quickly buried by Budhu's followers to avoid further brutalization.

This was just the beginning of the suppression of the Kol revolt, for the Company soldiers spared no one. Those in hiding—on trees, inside wells, under charpoys—were chased out and bayoneted. Not even women and children were spared, and infants clung on to their dead mothers, crying. The old women, including Budhu's sister-in-law, were imprisoned. One of Budhu's sons, Beni Bhagat, managed to escape.[8] What started as a battle had ended as a massacre. When the Company troops left, they carried away all the grains that had been stored and let the cattle loose.

### The aftermath of the 'Rock's' fall

With Budhu out of the picture, the British were relieved, as a major obstacle in their path to vanquishing the Kols had now been removed. Soon, the *mankis* and *mundas* of several Kol villages surrendered to Captain Impey, as expected. The encounter was vividly reported as 'A Khol (Kol) Killer' by the *Bengal Hurkaru and Chronicle* of Calcutta in its February 1832 edition. The correspondent described the cruel event as 'a jolly good drubbing' carried out in order to teach the Kols a lesson.[9]

---

[8]Ibid.
[9]Ibid.

However, the same correspontent confessed to being petrified at the sight of the decapitated heads of Budhu and his two followers. A rival paper gave it a sentimental twist by stating that 'Freedom shrieked when Budhu Bhagat fell'. It published a rather soul-stirring but imaginary 'last speech' given by Budhu in his final moments.[10]

However, as the Company troops speedily wrapped up their operations, it no longer mattered.

## Further changes in the Kol lifestyle

In total, 226 Hindus and 78 Muslims were killed; 4,086 houses were burnt; 17,058 cattle heads were seized and 822,992 mounds of grain were burnt across Chota Nagpur, as per the official records of the time.[11] This is not to say that the efforts of the Kols had gone to waste. Though late, Fort William did recognize that the ancient right to the land of the tribes of Chota Nagpur had to be respected and restored. In light of this, several administrative reforms were introduced by W. Dent and Captain Wilkinson, now appointed as Joint Commissioners of Chota Nagpur, to provide relief to the aggrieved tribes. So, Budhu Bhagat's supreme sacrifice was not in vain at all. In fact, it became a source of courage and inspiration for the survivors.

One of the first changes to be introduced was the abolition of the tax on *hanria*. This was widely welcomed as a conciliatory measure and made Captain Wilkinson popular. Further, he also befriended several Larka leaders after learning their language. By 1833, he was also holding durbars with the tribal folk. Soon, the bitterness was put aside and Captain Thomas Wilkinson came to be remembered as 'Al-Kisun Sahib'. Later, in 1834, when the South-West Frontier Agency was set up with its headquarters in

---
[10]Ibid.
[11]Macpherson, T.S. and M.G. Hallett, 'Bihar And Orisha District Gazetteers: Ranchi', Internet Archive, https://bit.ly/3uFzfqh. Accessed on 14 April 2022.

present-day Ranchi, Wilkinson was appointed as the first agent to serve the region. As he was familiar with the agrarian interests of the tribes, there was a general sense of security.

Unfortunately, though, no such shift occurred in the attitude of the rajas or the zamindars. Once the insurrection ended, they were back, not only in their homes but also to their earlier style of living off the hard work and wealth of the tribal folk. Exploitation continued in the form of land-grabbing, bonded and free labour.

## Fertile ground for the future

At the turn of the decade, in 1840, the tribes felt as if they were back to square one. Life was a continuous struggle to get back their legacy. Their desire to regain what was rightfully theirs was so strong that they were ready to do anything for it, at any cost. This proved to be quite advantageous to the German missionaries who arrived in Ranchi in 1844.

Sent by Father Johannes Evangelista Gossner from Berlin, a four-member missionary team started working in earnest from November 1845. By 1850, they had successfully converted four families belonging to the Oraon tribe living in the same region. The Oraons converted, firmly believing that it was the best possible option to tackle the oppressive zamindars and moneylenders. The new conflict over the possession of land took place between the Christianized tribes and the landlords, over the possession of land.

# 4
# U TIROT SING
## (1800–1833)
### The Broken Treaty of Friendship

In 1826, after ending the war with the Burmese through the Treaty of Yandaboo, the British secured Assam and were looking to strengthen political alliances in the region to thwart any future invasion by other imperialist forces. Under such circumstances, it was deemed necessary to have swift communication between Guwahati and Sylhet (at the time, it was part of Assam state), but the Khasi and Jaintia Hills came in the way. For David Scott, the then British political agent and commissioner of revenue and circuit in Assam, this was just a minor hurdle to overcome through negotiations. In fact, during his travels through Assam in 1824, having already noted the potential of a road from Nagaon to Sylhet, Scott had signed a treaty with U Ram Sing, the Jaintia king. Subsequently, he intended to do the same with the Khasi *syiems* (chiefs)— Bor Manik of Shillong, U Duwan of Sohra and U Konrai of Nongkhlaw, the latter being the principal state of the Khasi Hills. He also planned to get military assistance from these kings to fend off any further attacks by the Burmese. However, the East India Company's interest in the region was not purely motivated by political gains. Ever since they had gained control over Sylhet as a diwani from the Mughals in 1765 and commenced business there, they had heard of the lime quarries and other rich trade prospects in the Khasi Hills. So, mercantile interests were also very much at the fore of Scott's scheme of things but the idea was dormant then.

The Khasi and Jaintia kings were, on the contrary, worrying about the *dwars* (trade routes) of their kingdoms that passed through Assam and had been lost, first to the Burmese and then, to the British. These were the lifelines of those kingdoms, for it was through these routes that iron and limestone were exchanged for everyday utilities like rice, fish, salt, etc. With the trade routes lost, they were facing an economic crisis.

While the Syiem of Sohra, known for his anti-Nongkhlaw attitude, sided with Scott, the negotiations reached a deadlock in Shillong and came to a standstill in Nongkhlaw due to the death of U Konrai.

### The rise of Tirot Sing

Nongkhlaw, a village in the Nongstoin tehsil in the West Khasi Hills of Meghalaya spread from Bardwar in Kamrup, Assam, to Dewanganj and Rakhubir in present-day Bangladesh. It had given its people many illustrious kings who led by virtue and were victorious in their conquests. The kingdom also had a good track record of forming alliances with neighbouring states to successfully repulse invasions, be it from the Mughals or the Burmese. Now, the cause of the lost trade routes was uniting them again, under the new Syiem U Tirot Sing of Nongkhlaw.

Tirot Sing hailed from the royal family of Mawmluh, the centre of the iron industry and Nongkhlaw's seat of culture. His lineage was reputed for having fought off the British ever since their arrival in Sylhet. As a prince, Tirot was trained in warfare, games, languages, religion and the various administrative aspects of the kingdom. He ascended the throne in 1826 as per the matrilineal system of succession prevalent among the Khasis upon the death of U Konrai. Needless to say, he was well acquainted with the *dwar* issue.

Scott sought to continue his negotiations with the new Syiem. On 5 November 1826, at Tirot's inaugural durbar as the new Syiem, arriving with a party of officials, Scott distinguished himself by being the first British person to visit Nongkhlaw.[1]

In the absence of any regular road and for lack of any better mode of transport, Scott was carried by a couple of Garo mountaineers and then pulled by a powerful Toorkie horse for most of the journey. The exertion and the difficulty of his journey, which started on 1 November and took three days to finish, did nothing to thwart his spirits. As Scott left behind the heat- and malaria-ridden Brahmaputra Valley and climbed up into the cool, quiet balmy air of the hills with the snowy Himalayan ranges atop it, he added the construction of a sanatorium to his agenda as well.

## Happenings at the durbar

A day after Scott's arrival, Tirot Sing called a durbar. There were discussions on various subjects of mutual interest, but the discussions soon turned into a fiery debate led by fluent, fair-minded Khasi orators. Though highly impressed by the dignity, decorum and discipline of the Khasis, Scott had actually been looking for a quick discussion with the newly crowned king and moving on. Finally, after two days of intense debating, permission to construct the road and a sanatorium was granted. In return, Scott agreed to transfer the possession of Bardwar—the most strategic trade route for Nongkhlaw—to the Khasis. Scott celebrated the success of the negotiations by hosting a

---

[1]Bareh, Hamlet, *U. Tirot Singh,* Publications Division Ministry of Information & Broadcasting, 2017.

grand banquet and an archery contest.

This great bonhomie soon fell victim to Scott's expansionist ideas. The civil servant in Scott was driven by motives of conquest and enhanced revenue. By promoting the cultivation of European crops and mechanical arts, he firmly believed that he would be supplementing the efforts of the missionaries in 'civilizing' the hill people, for which the latter would feel gratitude. In fact, Scott himself had made it a point to distribute copies of the New Testament that had been translated to Assamese by the Baptist Mission, established in Cherrapunji. Later on, the first Bible was also published in the Khasi language to accelerate the spread of the gospel and increase conversions.

Meanwhile, the road survey proceeded under the guidance of Lieutenant Richard Gurdon Bedingfield and Lieutenant Philip Bowles Burlton, who were experts in discovering revenue-generating natural resources and constructing roads. However, with every passing day, it became evident that something wasn't right.

To begin with, Syiem Tirot found himself providing the workmen and money to construct the road—a point that hadn't even been discussed but had been written into the treaty by deceit and approved by the powers that be in Fort William. Next, there were increasing reports of the soldiers and sepoys, stationed at various spots to monitor the work, confiscating goods from the market, misbehaving with the women and ill-treating the villagers, including the labourers. Most importantly, there was no sign of Bardwar being returned to Syiem Tirot. The self-sustaining economy of the Khasis was getting replaced forcefully by an agrarian one, which wasn't doing them any good. There was no end in sight. To make matters worse, Scott sided with the Syiem's rival sitting 60 kilometres southwest of Nongkhlaw—the Raja of Rani—even providing him with troops to fight Syiem Tirot Sing.

## The honourable king

Like his contemporaries, Tirot Sing subscribed to a high moral code that had no room for covetousness, corruption or lust. He held fast to his word of honour and expected these sentiments to be reciprocated. On the contrary, Scott's attitude to their agreement was reflected in his downgrading of the Khasis from alliance partners to vanquished subjects, who only needed to be given a superficial impression of being treated equally.

This treachery did not sit well with Tirot Sing, and he convened another durbar to declare that the British must vacate with immediate effect. The durbar rejected this, stating that the only valid response under the circumstances was to battle it out. A few days later, these latent passions were fuelled further, when a Bengali peon at a local market let slip to a Khasi villager that Scott would subject them to taxation soon.

Accordingly, on 4 April 1829, under the pretext of participating in the durbar, Lieutenants Bedingfeld and Burlton were invited to Nongkhlaw. Upon their arrival, they were attacked. While Lieutenant Bedingfeld was killed on the spot, Lieutenant Burlton managed to escape with injuries. However, the hill warriors had anticipated this and were able to intercept him as he inched closer to Guwahati, where the Company had a light infantry in position. Sadly for him, before they could aid him, he was killed in an ambush.

Scott was away from Nongkhlaw, on a site inspection, when news of this massacre reached him. He couldn't see any reason for the Syiem to be displeased about anything and regarded the act as sheer madness on Tirot's part. To Scott, this whole incident was nothing more than an unwarranted skirmish. So, he just 'managed' it by dispatching a light infantry force under Captain F.J. Lister, who tried to discipline the hill warriors. It might have been a 'skirmish' for Scott, but for Tirot Sing, who regretted Scott's escape, it stoked the fire for an even-bloodier battle. While Scott worked to strengthen the British position with help from the *syiems* of Sohra and Rani, Tirot put together a strong alliance that aimed to ultimately overthrow Scott and his men with the help of *syiems* Bor Manik and U Muken of Mawsmai.

## A long battle commences

This was just the beginning of a long battle made difficult by the inequality of weaponry. The Khasi warriors were armed with bows, arrows and double-handed swords. A special regulation enforced by the Company in 1779 prohibited importing arms from Sylhet. This meant that the Khasi firearms were inferior to that of their enemy. The Khasis fought on the basis of their personal courage and martial skills as opposed to Captain Lister's force, which was used in modern warfare. The light infantry unit commanded by Lister was ruthless in its execution of the hill warriors. Even so, Tirot Sing managed to escape several times. Soon, Nongkhlaw was captured and Tirot Sing was declared an outlaw with the announcement of a reward of 1,000 rupees for his arrest. Simultaneously, reinforcements were sent under Captain Urquhart.

All this guerrilla warfare didn't impress Scott, who was himself quite skilled at it. The stately appearance of these warriors that had once charmed him and reminded him of the Roman heroes now only seemed to thoroughly disappoint him due to their lack of military discipline and invincibility.

If superior arms and ammunitions were Scott's strength, then it was Tirot Sing's personality and moral courage that came in the way of suppressing this insurrection—an aspect that even Scott respected. The Syiem was able to gather considerable support from his countrymen and other kings. This alliance survived until the movement collapsed.

Meanwhile, the location of the sanatorium was changed to Sohra (Cherrapunji) as it was found to be more accessible and suitable than Nongkhlaw while the road construction continued. The *syiems* of the states through which the road passed found themselves losing out power through treaties. Thus began a forceful shift of their allegiance to the government. Scott found this approach to be highly effective in breaking Tirot's alliance and isolating him. For instance, Bor Manik—who, along with U Muken, was Scott's top enemy—was captured through the dubious excuse of an interview with Scott to negotiate on the *dwars* that belonged to him. However, he managed to escape and continued to be a strong source of support to Tirot and a pain to the British.

## Attack at night

Come June 1830, there seemed to be no end to the 'skirmish' that had erupted some time ago. Using his strong diplomatic skills, Tirot Sing was able to count on the support of those who had solely chosen to believe in and stick with him, notably U Man Kumar—a mantri, U Lorshai Mairang—a sirdar and his cousin—U Jidor. He was also supported by his allies, including U Muken, U Ram Sing, U Phar, U Ksan, U Lar, U Khein Kongor and the Singphos whom he even visited personally despite the grave danger to his life.

Since Nongkhlaw was subjugated in 1829, Tirot Sing and his confederates shifted their base of operation to the Diengiei cave, known today as Ka Krem Tirot, where the remains of his military arsenal can still be seen. There, they planned new offensives to recapture the *dwars*, with terrorist methods, to wreak havoc on the government properties. Tirot had realized that fighting the British merely along the Assam and Sylhet borders wasn't going to be enough. The fight had to expand throughout the Northeast if they had to rattle them off. This call to unite brought in support from the villages of Rambrai, Nongkhlaw, Jymgam, Jirang, Nongstein, Boko, and the communities of the Garos,

Assamese, Rabhas, Lalungs, Mikirs and Shyams (Burmese volunteers). This new campaign was led by Syiem U Lorshon of Rambrai, Syiem U Roo of Boko and Syiem U Simtoo of Mookay, along with Tirot, his brother Subah, cousin Jidor and Mon Bhut, the most accomplished fighter in Tirot's camp.[2]

They struck on the night of 9 January 1831. Over the next one month, the *dwars* got occupied by the Khasis. None of Scott's existing military forces at these locations could do anything to stop Tirot Sing and his men. For once, the might of the modern British forces fell to the power of swords, arrows and spears. To bring matters under control, Scott sent Lieutenant David Hay Brodie. With his sadistic approach towards subjugating the masses, Brodie was able to turn the situation around but only until an arrow from the warrior camp struck his nose, which spelt a slow and severely painful death for him, and put the masses out of their misery.

## A losing battle

In the meantime, Tirot Sing started to lose his allies, including the *syiems* who had led the campaign to recapture the *dwars,* mainly because these smaller kingdoms, unable to bear the strain of the war, had gone broke and sought to salvage whatever remained by entering into a treaty with the British. This meant that they had to hand over certain key administrative and judicial powers to the government, along with unrestricted access to their iron and limestone quarries and a hefty sum as tribute. So, Tirot was now left with the support of only Bor Manik, Mon Bhut, his brothers and his cousins. He was disheartened that these allies could not muster the courage to stick to the very principles that they were fighting for. Adding to his distress were the daily reports of savagery inflicted by

---
[2]Ibid.

the troops, which were becoming too painful for him to bear—villages were rendered non-existent, crops were being burnt, villagers were starving and, having lost their possessions, were now living in the caves. Heavy fines were being imposed on whatever resources the Khasis were left with.

Meanwhile, the indefatigable Scott, who had been suffering from heart palpitations since his youth, had taken seriously ill, having developed jaundice, stomach ailments, difficulty in breathing and swollen legs. He died on 20 August 1831 at the age of 45 in Cherrapunji, spending his last days unable to eat or sleep.[3]

After Scott's death, Tirot was looking for an opportunity to strike again. In the November of 1831, a plan was hatched to strike at Sylhet. It was to be led by Mon Bhut—Tirot Sing's confidant and rumoured blacksmith who had a hand in the Nongkhlaw massacre—and U Subha Sing, Tirot's brother. Though they initially succeeded, they were eventually defeated by Captain Lister. By the beginning of 1832, Tirot, left with little resources and support, did not plan any more raids. Most significantly, he was deprived of his pillars of strength—Mon Bhut and Bor Manik. Tirot had to let go of Mon Bhut, who had killed another of Tirot's trusted men, while Bor Manik had temporarily departed to the plains in an attempt to rally more troops. The absence of Bor Manik cost Tirot Sing the most, though it was a matter of relief for the British, who considered him the most hostile warrior.

## Tough and long negotiations

Bor Manik's well-intentioned departure led to Deputy Syiem Sing Manik taking over Khyrim, which constituted one half of

---

[3]Watson, Archibald, *Memoir of the Late David Scott, Esq.*, Baptist Mission Press, 1832, p. 143.

Shillong.[4] In his new capacity as the Deputy Syiem, Sing Manik attempted to mediate between Tirot Sing and the British. Sing Manik had always been neutral towards the ongoing events, but he could foresee the disaster that awaited the remaining Khasi states if the war continued. This could be the reason why Tirot Sing was willing to consider his suggestion for an interview with the Company officials. Although, the extent to which Sing Manik had been genuine about his intentions towards Tirot Sing remains obscure, as he was generally regarded as a trusted friend of the British. This, however, could be the reason why the British government changed their earlier stand and adopted a diplomatic approach towards Tirot Sing. After much deliberation, Tirot agreed to a meeting with the government on 22 August 1832 at Nongkrem, but since the venue was a military tent, he refused to participate. He asked that it be shifted to Sing Manik's residence for the next day and that all parties come unarmed.

The next day, during the negotiations, Tirot Sing demanded that the sovereignty of his kingdom be restored, the construction of Scott's road be stopped or its route diverted and the British withdraw their presence once and for all. Captain Lister and Lieutenant H. Rutherford, who were representing the government, could not agree to these terms though they promised to restore him as the sovereign Syiem, based on the treaty of 1826. Needless to say, the negotiations reached no conclusion and the Syiem did not show up for further discussions the next day.

In September 1832, U Muken was tricked into surrendering and sent to Sylhet as a prisoner.

---

[4]Shillong consisted of Khyrim and Mylliem. There had been issues over succession between the syiems of these two regions, after which Bor Manik from the Mylliem lineage became the syiem. However, he had worked towards uniting the two parties. As a result, he appointed Sing Manik, who hailed from the Khyrim lineage, as the deputy syiem. The British took advantage of this during Bor Manik's absence and declared Khyrim independent of Bor Manik. It is believed that Bor Manik had consented to this.

In October, another truce with Tirot Sing was planned but the proposal was not very different from the one made in 1826. The rest of the year was spent negotiating and extending the deadline for accepting the truce. This suited the British because it gave them time to diplomatically ensure Tirot Sing's downfall by continuing to propose outrightly unacceptable terms while projecting themselves as the congenial party.

On 9 January 1833, Tirot Sing, while camping with his remaining followers near the Shillong peak, sent a message through his mantri, U Jit Roy, to Lieutenant H. Inglis, the commander of the post at Um Shyllong, of his readiness for an armistice. It was agreed that on 13 January, the Syiem would come to the British unarmed. However, on the appointed day, Tirot Sing showed up with 30 bowmen and 11 musketeers, in a bid to impress upon his subjects that although he had been in exile, he was still their heroic king who was heading for an amicable discussion with the warring party. For the armistice to be formalized, both Tirot Sing and Lieutenant Inglis agreed to lick salt off of a sword, as per the Khasi tradition, to keep their word. Tradition says that it was at this moment that Inglis rushed forward and arrested this brave son of Nongkhlaw. Records, however, state that the British took it as a sign of Tirot Sing's voluntary surrender and so Inglis had merely followed the protocol to take him as a prisoner of war.[5]

## The final trial

U Tirot Sing was tried at the Guwahati court, where he was sentenced to life imprisonment at Dacca, present-day Dhaka, Bangladesh. Later, he was treated as a political prisoner and entitled to a house, two servants and a monthly allowance of 63 rupees. Two years later, on 18 July 1835, S.C. Scott,

---
[5]Ibid.

the officiating magistrate at Dacca, wrote to the government secretary at Fort William, Calcutta, about the passing away of the former king at 1 p.m. the day before.

While the Anglo-Khasi War of 1829-33 came to an end with the capture of Tirot Sing. It also marked the start of the forward policy adopted by the British, according to which they aimed to control every inch of Northeast India. The Khasi Hills were now theirs. In 1835, they annexed the Jaintia Hills. The Garo people, divided about supporting Tirot, were eventually captured in 1869. This is not to say that Tirot's efforts were nullified. In fact, Tirot is credited with being the first king in this part of India who put up a united fight against foreign occupation. If one considers Tirot's fight as unfinished business, then one may take heart in the fact that even after his capture, Syiem U Sngap Sing of Maram (known today as Maharam) kept the embers of this war glowing by single-handedly fighting the British till 1839.

Sadly, due to the misguided notions of the Welsh missionaries, who filled in the gap left by the departure of the Baptist Mission, the Khasis and the Jaintias were gradually isolated and cut off from having any understanding of Tirot Sing or even their own culture.

Around 120 years later, on 29 March 1954, in the serene valley of Mairang, a town near Nongkhlaw, a memorial was erected in honour of Tirot Sing. It is a reminder of what he stood for, felt and did for his motherland, though he may have breathed his last far away from her. The epitaph dedicated to him reads:

*This is my own my native land, the land consecrated with the blood of my ancestors.*[6]

---

[6]English translation of the epitaph of U Tirot Sing at Mairang, quoted in Bareh, Hamlet, *U. Tirot Singh*, Publications Division Ministry of Information & Broadcasting, 2017.

# 5

# SIDHU, KANHU, CHAND AND BHAIRAB

(unknown–1856)

## Brothers on a Quest for Justice

In August 1854, two aggrieved Santhal village chiefs, Nursingh Manjhi and Koondru Manjhi, petitioned against the extortionist mahajans (moneylenders) to the commissioner at Bhagalpur.[1] Despite being less educated, by filing a petition, Nursingh and Koondru had done what no Santhals had dared to do before—raise their voice against the injustice meted out to them. But the matter wasn't so straightforward. The two chiefs would have to get past the corrupt clerks, pleaders, peons and guards before their petition reached the commissioner.

Nursingh and Koondru submitted a long list of grievances, the first being the replacement of the barter system with a cash-based economy. The simple-minded Santhals, uninitiated in this new system, found themselves borrowing from the mahajans and repaying the loan at a high interest rate that often led to them losing their harvest to the moneylenders. Quite often, the mahajans used to quickly file a suit against the Santhals

---

[1] Xalxo, Abha, 'The Great Santal Insurrection (Hul) of 1855-56', *Proceedings of the Indian History Congress*, Vol. 69, 2008, pp. 732–755.

in the court, with the latter only finding out about when the court decree arrived ordering the sale of their cattle, home, vessels and ornaments. Traditionally, the peasants would have complained to their manjhi, or the head man, of their hamlet. These manjhis would, in turn, dispense justice. The people had complete faith in the manjhis as well as in their system of justice. But with this new system, they found themselves powerless because the British government controlled everything.

Further, the British judge had little time to spare for what he perceived to be 'petty' grievances. As long as the revenue was coming in, there was nothing amiss in his books and reports on the region. His immediate focus was on the work that needed to be done on the railway line that would run from Tinpahadia to Rajmahal Hills, through the Damin-i-Koh to Bhagalpur, Bihar. The Santhals had been roped in to work here as cultivators and day labourers. The wages were good. Surely, the British thought, there was nothing more the Santhals could ask for. Unfortunately for the British, there was.

## A worsening system of justice

As the months passed by and there was no response to the manjhis' petition, the angry and disappointed Santhals resorted to robbing the mahajans and zamindars under the enthusiastic leadership of Bir Singh, the manjhi of Lachimpur village. To bring the situation under control, the daroga (police inspector) from the nearby town of Burhait, Mahesh Lal Dutta, was sent. The Daroga brutally beat up Bir Singh and his followers in order to break their spirit. For some time, the Santhals were quiet and stolidly bore the misdeeds of the moneylenders. Among those who had been wronged and chose not to say anything at the moment was Chunar Murmu, the manjhi of Bhognadih village, which lay to the south of Burhait. Murmu had been deceived into losing both his land and house to the zamindars. Murmu and his four sons—Kanhu, Sidhu, Chand and Bhairab—were well respected in their community as warriors. Santhal villages far and near grew alarmed at the suffering that had befallen Chunar Murmu due to the usury of the mahajans. This wasn't the deal that they had signed up for.

Following the famine of 1770 and the Permanent Settlement Act of 1793, the Santhals had arrived at the Damin-i-Koh after being wrung out by the tax-hungry zamindars. They had come to regard the Damin-i-Koh as their promised land, where they could live peacefully and preserve their identity. However, to the British, they were exactly the set of people whose expertise in clearing forest lands and cultivation would be financially beneficial. The Damin was government property, and so, the cultivated lands would bring in more tax from the zamindars. However, Santhals seldom paid rent, apart from the price that their manjhis had bargained with the zamindars. In fact, whole villages migrated when the British demanded rent to allow the Santhals to cultivate their land.

Ever since the Bir Singh episode, mass gatherings were viewed with suspicion. Yet, the Santhals understood that it was important for them to meet and discuss the way forward. So, the Murmu brothers started gathering Santhal youths—under the pretext of traditional group hunting and planning propitiatory rituals to ward off mythical snakes that devoured humans—to discuss their unfavourable situation and united them. During these meetings, several injustices that had remained hidden since then came to light: when merchants from far and near flocked to the weekly markets at Burhait at the heart of the Damin to purchase large quantities of rice, butter and mustard, they used heavy weights to ascertain the purchase. Much of this was then exported to England. However, they paid the Santhals in cash, salt, tobacco or cloth, using lighter weights to determine the return.

Realizing that unlike their own system for justice, the

government wasn't going to give them a fair hearing, the Murmu brothers decided to take matters into their own hands but still sought divine intervention.

Sidhu, the eldest of the siblings and the most spiritual of the four, went into deep prayer and meditation. Tradition claims that this resulted in several visits by Thakur, a Santhal deity. Several times, Thakur appeared to Sidhu in his dreams and, after instructing him that the time had come for ousting the *dikus*, he 'ascended and disappeared'.[2] Soon, Thakur started appearing before Kanhu's brothers as well. It is believed that for nearly seven consecutive days, the Thakur's visitations continued in various forms, including that of a book, knife, cartwheel and fire. Convinced by this divine intervention, Kanhu and Sidhu built a statue of Thakur in their garden and began spreading his message by passing sal branches, the traditional mode of communication for important messages among the Santhals. At a gathering of 10,000 Santhals, Kanhu formally conveyed the message from Thakur, which was instantly accepted. It was proclaimed that Sidhu was their king; Kanhu, the adviser; Chand, the administrator; and Bhairab, the commander. It was agreed that an ultimatum would be issued to the daroga, mahajans, zamindars and the British sahibs to address the existing grievances and then move out. If no reply was received within 15 days, there would be war.

## The commencement of the Santhal *hul*

On 30 June 1855, with the call of '*Hul! Hul!*' Kanhu and Sidhu, led a group of 10,000 Santhal youths, and attacked the traders and the mahajans at the local market at Bhognadih. About a dozen people were killed. A week later, on 7 July, Sidhu killed

---

[2] Quoted in Gott, Richard, *Britain's Empire: Resistance, Repression and Revolt*, Verso, London, 2011.

Daroga Mahesh Lal Dutta, who had been sent once again to subdue the disturbance. Sidhu was avenging the death of Bir Singh; it was revenge in its purest form, and he made no efforts to hide it. The next day, the Santhals, led by the Murmu brothers, reached Pakur, which was a stronghold of the zamindars. Here, the four brothers entered the house of the richest zamindar, Gode Madan Mohan, but were disappointed to find that he had escaped with his family, taking all the valuables with him. They held the town under siege for the next three days, during which they plundered the surrounding villages.

Under Chand and Bhairab's leadership, one group of Santhals advanced towards Murshidabad, where they attacked the indigo factory on 14 July. However, they were fought off by a party of around 200 guards of the magistrate. Consequently, the group started burning down the railway bungalows and destroyed all the construction that had been carried out until then. Many Englishmen and two English ladies were killed. When Sidhu learnt of this, he condemned the act and rebuked his younger brothers, insisting that a certain code of conduct must be observed in their fight that was being divinely guided. This meant sparing the lives of those who had not exploited the Santhals.

So far, the *hul* had not met with any serious resistance. This was mainly due to the absence of any British troops in the immediate vicinity that could quickly reach the area of disturbance and suppress the uprising. Actually, the government had not expected the peace-loving Santhals to turn restive to the point of aiming their bows and arrows at them. Owing to this ignorance, the British realized quite late and much to their bewilderment, the stage had been set for a protracted rebellion. As part of this, the Santhals had taken possession of Burhait, which became their headquarters. The Murmu brothers were carried about in palanquins as though they had become the new masters of the land.

Finally, on 15 July, the 7th Native Infantry led by Major Charles Shuckburgh was dispatched from Berhampore by the magistrate of Murshidabad. They were met by Sidhu and Kanhu when they were halfway to the Damin-i-Koh. A fight erupted in which both Sidhu and Kanhu were injured and over 200 Santhals were killed. In retaliation, Shuckburgh's troops burned down the village of Bhognadih and reclaimed Burhait. Simultaneously, the Commissioner of Bhagalpur, D.F. Brown, dispatched a body of hill rangers under Major F.W. Burroughs to address the situation. The troops were fiercely attacked by the Santhals under the leadership of Chand and Bhairab at Pirpainti and were eventually defeated on 16 July. Highly embarrassed and shocked by this, the Commissioner requested Major General Llyod, posted at Dinapur, for more troops. About a week later, on 25 July, he also sought to impose martial law. Five days later, Fort William retracted its order, deeming the Commissioner's request as illegal. In the meantime, the cry of *hul* reached Birbhum and Hazaribagh, where the fighters stormed the jail and set it afire.

In early August 1855, A.C. Bidwell, who was the commissioner of Nadia, was appointed as a special commissioner to suppress the rebellion. He issued a proclamation asking the Santhals to surrender and assuring pardon to all except the leaders. In a meeting convened by Kanhu, this offer was rejected. Hereafter, close to 30,000 Santhals, including women and children, started marching towards Calcutta to present their petition to Governor General Lord Dalhousie. In the course of their journey, they hunted down every Mahajan in their sight. Already, the Santhals had closed in on Calcutta by fighting their way against the troops stationed at every river along the Grand Trunk Road. In other places, they demolished the telegraph, post and railway operations.

## Consequences of armed war

In preparing to fight the *dikus*, neither Kanhu nor Sidhu had considered the consequences of facing the British rifles. Both trusted the blessings of their deity to see them through. However, this lack of knowledge about the damage that the British sahibs' weaponry could cause did frighten the other Santhals who were armed only with traditional bows, arrows and axes. The method of fighting by invoking their deity worked well when fighting the mahajans and zamindars but combating a force armed with modern weaponry was proving to be a challenge. It was only Chand's persuasion that helped them overcome their trepidation. Major Vincent Jervis, who had been specially ordered in from Barrackpore with his troops by the commissioner of Burdwan to suppress the insurrection, took advantage of this fear and ordered for a blank volley to be fired on the Santhals. This convinced the Santhals that the bullets weren't deadly and, in return, the British troops found that the arrows of the Santhals were non-poisonous. This was followed by the first of the many deceitful tactics of the British—they fired live rounds on the Santhals. As the Santhals ran to escape, many got swept away or drowned in the river on the banks of which the battle was fought. Major Shuckburgh then destroyed the Santhals' properties.

On 19 August, Bhagna, a close aide of the Murmu brothers, betrayed Sidhu. Tying him up in cords under the pretext of applying medicine to his wounds, he delivered Sidhu to Major Shuckburgh's camp at Gutirai, a little-known place a few miles away from Bhagalpur. Sidhu was then taken to Bhagalpur for a trial and was hanged publicly at Burhait. The traitor was mercilessly cut to pieces by Sidhu's followers. In Hazaribagh, British troops, with the support of the Raja of Ramgarh and his jagirdars, suppressed the insurrection by burning down Santhal villages. Undefeated, the Santhals sought and received support from the many non-tribal communities—ironsmiths, milkmen, oilers, barbers and Doms.[3] Another prominent feature of this rebellion was the active participation of women led by Phulo Murmu and her sister Jhano Murmu, who belonged to Pakur. They were even sent to jail.

## Crushing the rebellion

Sidhu's capture by treachery and his consequent martyrdom were both a blow to the movement as well as an inspiration and a motivating force. In September 1855, as directed by Kanhu, Bhairab captured a dak-runner on the way to Birbhum and asked him to deliver a sal branch to the magistrate, failing which he was threatened with dire consequences. This was a warning to the government. The leaves on the branch indicated the number of days until the Santhals attacked the town—there were three. As the civil and military officers at Birbhum debated their action plan, their three days were up and they found themselves plundered, as forewarned.

On 10 November, martial law was declared in Bhagalpur, Murshidabad and Birbhum. With this began the most brutal phase of suppression of the rebellion. British troops along with the zamindars, Ghatwals,[4] police, indigo planters and the nawab of Murshidabad, raided and destroyed Santhal property. They combed the forested region to get hold of every single Santhal, and any Santhal in sight was court-martialled. As Major Jervis

---

[3]This is a Bengali Hindu caste that was classified as a criminal tribe under the Criminal Tribes Act 1871. It was repealed in August 1949 and replaced with the Habitual Offenders' Act in 1952.
[4]Chiefs of the feudal land granted under the zamindari system. They were found only in the Santhal regions (later Santhal Parganas). They were mainly responsible for maintaining law and order. Every estate had its own armed force.

later opined to Sir William Wilson Hunter,[5] author of *Annals of Rural Bengal*, the brutal suppression had stopped being a war by that time.[6] It was plain and simple execution, and there was no end in sight. It was an unequal war, what with the modern weapons of the British troops pitted against the reckless courage of the Santhals.

In December 1855, the magistrate of Birbhum identified the twelve Santhal leaders who needed to be captured dead or alive. The remaining three Murmu brothers topped this list. Most of these leaders were caught by the first week of January 1856 and martial law was withdrawn. Kanhu was caught in February near Banda by Sardar Ghatwal of Kunjra. Along with Chand, Bhairab and others, he was sentenced to death and hanged. Most of their followers were sentenced to long-term imprisonment ranging from seven to 14 years.

## The impact of the *hul*

As the *hul* ended, Ashley Eden, who later went on to become the lieutenant governor of Bengal, launched an enquiry to understand why this uprising had come as a surprise. Much to the astonishment of the government, its officers realized that the Santhals were right—there was no effective means of dispensing justice and the economy did consist of administering taxes without offering anything substantial in return. Based on these findings, the Sonthal Parganas Act (Act XXXVII) of 1855 was introduced. The Act consolidated the Santhal areas into a separate non-regulation district—the Santhal Parganas. This area was separated from the districts of Bhagalpur and Birbhum

---

[5]Sir William Wilson Hunter KCSI CIE was a Scottish historian, statistician, a compiler and a member of the Indian Civil Service, best known for producing *The Imperial Gazetteer of India*.
[6]Hunter, William Wilson, *Annals of Rural Bengal*, Smith, Elder and Company, United Kingdom, 1871.

and divided into four sub-districts—Dumka, Deoghar, Godda and Rajmahal (including Pakur). Eden went on to become the first deputy commissioner of Santhal Parganas, after which he introduced the Police Rules of 1856, which invested the manjhis of the Santhal villages with police powers that they could exercise in their villages, assisted by the village chowkidar.

Thus, the law was catching up with the fraudulent moneylenders who asked for the same debt to be paid twice or thrice; bonded labour and slavery ended; the use of false weights and measures were kept in check and the Santhals were finally able to sell their produce with the assurance of not being cheated. Most importantly, this rebellion unified the Santhals living across Damin-i-Koh and the newly minted Santhal Parganas in their quest to build their promised land and protect their cultural identity. This vision served as the foundation for the next wave of the freedom struggle under Birsa Munda.

# 6

## BABURAO SHEDMAKE
(1833–1858)

## AND RAMJI GOND
(1830–1860)

Young, Unhappy Kings in the City of Moon

Until the middle of the eighteenth century, the region between the present-day Chandrapur district of Maharashtra and the Adilabad district of Andhra Pradesh was known as Gondwana. The region lay between the Narmada and Godavari rivers and was divided into four kingdoms—Garha in the north; Deogarh and Kherla in the centre; and Chanda in the south. These independent kingdoms were ruled by a branch of the Gond dynasty, whose origins remain unclear. However, by matching secondary sources with the details recorded in the *Ain-i-Akbari*, the third volume of the *Akbarnama*, it has been largely accepted that the Chanda dynasty came into being around 1240 in Sirpur and was established by Bhim Ballal Shah. The Chanda rulers were known to be valiant fighters and even fought against the Rajputs on behalf of the Delhi sultans.[1]

---

[1] Bhukya, Bhangya, 'The Subordination of the Sovereigns: Colonialism and the Gond Rajas in Central India, 1818–1948', *Modern Asian Studies*, Vol. 47, No. 1, 2013, pp. 288–317.

## Sher Shah and Raghoji

The Gond king Surja Ballal Singh won the title of 'Sher Shah' from the Sultan upon a battle victory. This title was passed on to his descendants who added the suffix 'Shah' to their names. Good relations prevailing between Delhi and Chanda meant that the Chanda rulers never paid any tribute to the sultans while enjoying full rights to maintain an army with a cavalry of 10,000 soliders and an infantry of 40,000 soliders. True to the Chanda insignia of a crested griffin destroying an elephant, it was a prosperous kingdom. However, trouble was brewing on the horizon in the form of Raghoji Bhonsle I, the Maratha warrior who had ruled Bihar since 1737.

Raghoji Bhonsle I had conquered the Deogarh kingdom in 1743 by cleverly manoeuvring his way through the succession issues upon the death of the Deogarh king. In doing so, he had also crossed swords with the other Gond kingdoms, including Chanda. The other kingdoms did not take this lightly. Sporadic attacks broke out on both the Gond and Maratha sides, which eventually developed into a full-scale war with the kingdom of Chanda in 1749. The war lasted for four months, at the end of which the then Gond king of Chanda, Nilkanth Shah, was defeated by Raghoji Bhonsle I.[2] Nilkanth Shah was captured, imprisoned and his kingdom brought under Bhonsle rule. Under the rule of the Marathas, Chanda became an autonomous zamindari instead of an independent kingdom. The King and other chieftains lost their political power and were reduced to the rank of ordinary zamindars. However, they were allowed to carry out raids in the forests and hills as well as the neighbouring regions that actually came under the jurisdiction of the Nizam of Hyderabad. These raids helped the Gond kings maintain whatever remained of their social status

---

[2]Ibid.

and sovereignty and keep a check on the natural resources. In fact, the Gonds of Chanda had found a place of favour with Appa Saheb, the last Maratha king of Nagpore (now Nagpur), who regarded Chanda as a place of strategic importance in keeping out the British. So, he had maintained an army of Gonds and a garrison at the Chanda Fort. He had found support in Bhujang Rao, the zamindar of Ahiri and his brother Kondu Bapu, the zamindar of Arpalli.

## Change of guards

The British arrived in the region close on the heels of the Marathas. Towards the end of the third, and final, Anglo-Maratha War (1817–1819), the British broke the Maratha supremacy in the Central Provinces by defeating Bhujang Rao, who led his Gond army in a brave fight against them. With the fall of Chanda on 2 May 1818, the British victory was complete and Nagpore became a British protectorate. Appa Saheb was deposed and replaced by his adopted heir—Bajiba, the 10-year-old son of Banu Bai, one of Raghoji II's daughters. Once Bajiba had been adopted as the heir apparent on 26 June 1818, he was renamed Raghoji III and appointed as the new ruler by the British Resident Richard Jenkins. In 1826, when Raghoji III turned 18, the Resident handed over the administration to him and sealed a treaty with him as per which Chanda, Chattisgarh and Devgad would be under the British jurisdiction.

On 11 December 1853, at 6.00 a.m., Raghoji III, aged 47 years, died after a period of prolonged illness. Even though he had not left behind an heir to the throne, the royal family was convinced that, like the previous time, an heir would be adopted this time around as well. Sadly, and to their great shock, this did not happen. Instead, the then Resident G.C. Mansel was directed by the office of the Governor General Lord Dalhousie to not encourage any such initiative until further notice, which came on 7 March 1854. In it, Mansel received the orders to annex Nagpore. With the annexation, Chanda received its first deputy commissioner, R.S. Ellis of the Madras Civil Service, on 18 December 1854.

## An unhappy king in Chanda

The annexation completely transformed the manner in which the state of Nagpore had been administered until then. One of the first signs was the setting up of the telegraphic services in the region, with the Calcutta–Bombay line being laid in 1854–1855. As the British sense of modernity proliferated in the region, it caused discontentment among the masses and the erstwhile rulers for whom these changes were alien and difficult to comprehend. When news of the annexation reached Chanda, a cry for revolution against the British was raised among the zamindars, who saw this as their opportunity to win back their independence. In this scenario, the revolt of 1857 was a godsend. However, stringent policing, extensive disarming of civilians and armed forces alike and extreme precautionary measures ensured that the devil's wind only blew like a breeze through the region.

A few of the Gond kings were unhappy about this lost opportunity. One of them was 25-year-old Baburao Shedmake, the Gond king of the Molampalli zamindari of Chanda. He was the eldest son of Poolaisur Bapu and Jurja Kunwar. Born on 12 March 1833 at Kishtapur village in Gadchiroli district, Baburao started his education at the age of three, initially at the Ghotul Sanskar Kendra, where he was taught Hindi, Gondi and Telugu along with martial arts, music and dance. Later, he was sent to the British-run English-medium institution in Raipur, Chattisgarh, to receive a western education. Upon his return to Molanpalli, he was married to Raj Kunwar, who belonged to the Madavi royal family of Chennur in the Adilabad district. A year later, in mid-1857, the mutiny broke out, and he felt that the Gonds had failed to capitalize on it.

## A revolt breaks out

However, encouraged by the mutiny of 1857, Baburao started his own preparations to fight the British. He was joined by Venkat Rao, the zamindar of Arpalli and Ghot. Together, they raised an army of 500 youths belonging to the Gond, Maria and Rohilla tribes, called the 'Jangom Sena', and launched their campaign at Rajghad of that same year. On 24 September 1857, word of this attack reached then Deputy Collector Captain William H. Crichton, who sent an army to contain it. Crichton, formerly a lieutenant with the 38th Regiment of Madras Native Infantry, was familiar with the ground realities and politics of Nagpore, having served as the superintendent of police and bazaars and postmaster for Nagpore since November 1853. Despite his experience, he was defeated when Baburao's army intercepted the British army near Nandgaon–Ghosari on 13 March 1858.

Emboldened by the two victories, the Gond kings increased the strength of their army to 1,200 men and proceeded to Chunchgondi, one of the largest villages of the Ahiri zamindari estate, situated on the banks of the Pranhita River. Chunchgondi was an important location for the British, as their telegraph office was located there. Seeking to derail the functioning of the British administration, Baburao ordered an attack on the office. On the night of 29 April, the entire office was destroyed, and two of its employees, Gartland and Hall, were killed. A third employee, Peter, however, managed to escape to Ahiri town. Luckily for him, Captain Crichton was present there, overseeing the military operations.[3] Upon

---

[3]Ibid.

arrival, he notified Crichton about the fate that had befallen them at Chunchgondi.

The deputy collector finally comprehended the extent of the danger that Baburao and Venkat Rao were capable of unleashing. He also realized that this wasn't a fight he could win by himself. In consultation with Captain Henry John Childe Shakespear, who commanded the Nagpore Irregular Force, he decided to involve Laxmi Bai, the zamindarini of Ahiri. Asking Peter to dress himself up as a native, Crichton directed him to make his way to the Ahiri palace and deliver a letter to Laxmi Bai, seeking her support in squashing the Gond kings' army. To the captain's relief, she agreed. What he wasn't aware of was that she was hand in glove with Baburao and Venkat Rao as well. Bolstered by this seemingly newfound alliance with Laxmi Bai, Captain Crichton proceeded to attack Chanda. However, just as his army entered the hills of the region, their advance was abruptly halted by the Gond army's guerilla warfare. The skilful arrow and stone shots of the Gond soldiers, along with their time-tested approach of blocking passes by felling trees, were enough to defeat Crichton's force.

A much-frustrated Captain Crichton returned to Nagpore with the intention of never going back to Chanda. But he wasn't giving up either. He announced cash awards of 1,000 rupees each for the heads of Baburao and Venkat Rao, in the hope that someone among the petty chiefs, lured by the money, would come forward to assist him. This did not happen because Baburao and Venkat Rao's army was built and sustained by the financial and material resources supplied by these small-time chiefs. In fact, it was due to their support that the Gond revolt expanded to the nearby Wardha and the northern regions of Hyderabad, where the zamindars, Rohillas and Arabs openly supported their cause. Their leader was Ramji Gond, who ruled over Nirmal, Utnoor, Chennuru and Asifabad—all part of the present-day Adilabad district.

The failure of the reward scheme raised questions in Captain Crichton's mind about Laxmi Bai's support. In the absence of any evidence, he started threatening her that should she be found supporting the Gond army, she would be deprived of her estate. Ahiri, at that point, was going through a rough time due to the support extended to the warring parties. There was an immense scarcity of food. Taking into consideration the welfare of her subjects, Laxmi Bai visited Crichton in person at Nagpore and assured him both verbally and in writing that she would arrest Venkat Rao within a few days and Baburao in a couple of months. In return, Crichton arranged the supply of cattle fodder and food grains for her estate.

## A twist in the tale

Upon her return to Ahiri, Laxmi Bai wrote to Crichton that Venkat Rao had been caught. However, she would be willing to hand him over only if she could be assured that he would only be imprisoned and not hanged, as he was a relative. Also, she wanted his estates to be transferred to her. Her final condition was that since she had already spent 1,200 rupees to catch Venkat Rao and needed another 4,000 rupees to capture Baburao, she should be sent this money immediately. Crichton refused all of these conditions. He responded that if Laxmi Bai did not hand over Venkat Rao unconditionally, then he would imprison her and her estate would be forfeited.

Unfazed by the threat, Laxmi Bai held her ground. Soon, news emerged that Venkat Rao had escaped from her custody. Crichton was now convinced that this was Laxmi Bai or Baburao's doing. Laxmi Bai defended herself, stating that since she was busy with her daughter's wedding, it wasn't possible for her to be involved in such activities. Again, in the absence of evidence, there wasn't much that Crichton could do.

## Betrayal or a friendship honoured?

The months sped by, and, with the onset of the monsoon, Crichton's plans of rounding up his nemesis went on hold again. Baburao took advantage of the situation. Although the strength of his army had come down to 200, it was still large enough to systematically keep wreaking havoc at the various military outposts. Frustrated but undaunted, Crichton persevered as well. Knowing well that Laxmi Bai was going to be his key to capturing Baburao, he continued with his threats. This plan eventually worked. On 18 September 1858, Laxmi Bai invited Baburao and Venkat Rao for dinner. However, the invite turned out to be a ploy to have her servants hand them over to the British. While Baburao was handed over to Crichton, Venkat Rao managed to escape to Bastar, from where he continued his raids. It wasn't until April 1860 that he was arrested by the Raja of Bastar and handed over to the British.

Despite the coldness and differences between Laxmi Bai and Captain Crichton, she was rewarded with 67 villages from Venkat Rao's Ghot and Arpalli zamindari estates. Also, at her request, Venkat Rao was only sentenced to life imprisonment. However, no such leniency was shown towards Baburao. He was sent to the Chanda Central jail for trial. The hearing was scheduled for 21 October 1858, during which he was sentenced to death by hanging. The order was promptly carried out at 4.30 p.m. the same day. Both Captains Crichton and Shakespear were present for it.

## A legacy continued

While Captain Crichton could finally heave a sigh of relief, there was no such luxury for his counterpart in Hyderabad, thanks to the raids by Ramji Gond. Colonel Cuthbert Davidson, the British Resident at Hyderabad, had been feeling much-harassed by the Gond chief's incessant attacks. Even though the mutiny of 1857 had been contained in Adilabad, anti-British sentiments were still prevalent in the region, which found favour with the disgruntled Rohillas and Arabs who had been disbanded from military service and had settled in this region. The local petty Gond chiefs were only adding to the troubles of these raids.

In the aftermath of Nagpore's conversion into a British protectorate, the British and the Gond kings and chiefs agreed that they should mutually respect and honour each other. By 1854, when the annexation was complete, this agreement had been dissipated. The written treaty was also breached as per which the Gond kings and chiefs would not raid the forests, hills and British territories. The anger, revolt and raids of the Gonds were, thus, justified.

In the case of Hyderabad, Ramji Gond's repeated raids had called for constant surveillance by the 47th Regiment of the Bengal Native Infantry along with a detachment of the subsidiary force under Colonel Roberts being posted there.

Finally, on 1 April 1860, the British got some relief. Just after 4.00 a.m. that day, the collector of the Nirmal district received information that Ramji had rounded up his army in the mountainous locations on the outskirts of Nirmal. The collector knew that it was geographically impossible to access the place and logistically impossible for the British troops to survive. Yet, driven by a sense of duty and patriotism, he left for the place accompanied by a troop, reaching there by midday. Soon, intense hostility broke out between the two groups. What started with firing ended with sword fights. Hundreds of rebels were killed. Many of the injured fled. The rest were arrested and imprisoned. Yet, Ramji Gond could not be found.

It would be another six months before a worried Colonel Davidson enquired into the matter again. In those intervening months, Davidson had spent his time persuading the Nizam of Hyderabad to support the British in eliminating Ramji

Gond. While records are not very clear about who eventually captured him, we are able to infer that he was arrested and sentenced to capital punishment around 17 September 1860, at Nirmal.

Eighty years later, another Gond leader, Komaram Bheem, was also executed by shooting in retaliation to his fight for the Gonds' rights to their forests, land and water.

# 7

## TANTYA BHIL

(1842–1889)

### The Village's Uncle: From Beloved to Betrayed

In 1866, after the Great Indian Peninsular Railways opened the Bhusaval–Khandwa section of the Howrah–Allahabad–Mumbai line, the railway staff at the Khandwa junction frequently found themselves telegraphing their headquarters about their station master being carried away or attacked by tigers or leopards. For a decade, this situation prevailed, causing inconvenience and fear. Then, starting April 1879, an entity far scarier in its ways of execution than wild cats arrived at the scene—a badmash named Tantya made Khandwa the centre of his activities. The Khandwa bazaar and railway route were his ideal targets. Not a train could pass through these areas without being robbed by Tantya and his gang. After they had looted enough, they would distribute the goods among the needy and keep the rest for themselves. While this gave Tantya a messiah-like reputation among the oppressed masses, it gave the entire British administration bad press for being unable to defend their railways, their lifeline in the most economically important part of their empire. What made it even more humiliating was that after every episode of robbery and loot, the police would arrive only to find no trace of where the bandits had come from or escaped to.

## Early years

Tantya had not always been a badmash nor had he intended to become one. Tantya was born in 1842 into the Bhil community of Barda (or Badada) village of the present-day Pandhana tehsil, Khandwa district, Madhya Pradesh. His parents were Bhau Singh, a farmer, and his wife. Tantya grew up assisting his father. Though lanky in appearance, Tantya possessed tremendous physical strength, even as a child. His strength was proven when his village had been attacked by a wild buffalo that had gone berserk. Tantya, then barely a teen, effortlessly and fearlessly held the animal by its horns and whipped it into submission. Despite his extraordinary strength, Tantya never came across as a troublemaker or someone who would take undue advantage of his physical capabilities. Villagers regarded him as a mild-mannered, helpful and friendly boy.

All this changed once his father, Bhau Singh, died. Until his father's passing in 1874, Tantya and Bhau Singh had been living as tenants and farming on a piece of land in Pokhar town. After Bhau's death, Tantya approached Shiva and Sardar Patel, the zamindars who owned this piece of land, with the hopes of continuing to receive patronage from them. Instead, Shiva told him that he no longer had any right to the land he had been tilling. Angered at this injustice and humiliation, Tantya rounded up Shiva and his men and chased them out of Pokhar. Shiva swore vengeance and, being a zamindar, all he had to do to carry out his revenge was report Tantya to the police, who were allies of the zamindars. Soon enough, the police declared Tantya a badmash and arrested him. Tantya was 32 then.

## An unhappy interlude and banditry

After serving a sentence of a year of rigorous imprisonment at the Nagpore Central jail, Tantya returned to Pokhar hoping to improve his life. However, this was not to be. Shiva Patel was unhappy and angry at Tantya's return. The situation became worse when he learnt that Tantya was in love with Shiva's daughter, Jasoda.[1] To address this situation, Shiva falsely implicated Tantya in a robbery that took place in the neighbouring village of Hirapur. Tantya was arrested along with Bijnia, a criminal. Though their offence was never proven, the court sent both of them to jail. Tantya was lodged at the Jubbalpore jail while Bijnia was kept in the Khandwa jail. They had been friends before they were sent to jail, and their friendship continued following their release after serving a sentence of three months of rigorous imprisonment.

Wanting to start life afresh, Tantya shifted to Seora, which was being ruled by Maharaja Tukoji Rao Holkar II of Indore, expecting to be out of sight of the Pokhar zamindars. However, Shiva Patel, to exact revenge, kept an eye on Tantya when he was in the Holkar territory as well. Fed up with the vicious cycle of conflicts with the police and zamindars and with no hope for justice, Tantya finally decided to live in the forest, looting and thieving for a living. To his relief and surprise, he soon attracted sympathizers. These were simple folk who had lost their property and respect at the hands of zamindars. They bonded well and soon turned into a gang that was out to punish the evil zamindars. His chief lieutenants were Bijnia and Daulia.

Although Tantya chose to be a dacoit, his morals were intact. For instance, he never harmed women and children. Once, while attacking a zamindar's house, the wife offered him her ornaments, as her husband was away. Tantya refused to accept them. Another time, Tantya ran into a wedding and asked to be taken to meet the bride and groom, and gifted

---

[1] This and most of the historical facts about Tantya's life mentioned in this chapter have been taken from Mukherjee, Charu Chandra, *The Life of Tantia Bhil: The Renowned Bandit-Chief,* B.H. Dutt, Calcutta, 1890.

cash to both of them. Once, he heard that Jasoda was being harassed by Sardar Patel's widow and daughter, who refused to return the money they had borrowed from Jasoda. Tantya promptly showed up at the Patel residence, looted their precious household articles and, dragging the widow and her daughter by their hair, left them at the outskirts of the village with their noses cut. These avuncular and saviour-like attributes of Tantya's personality made the villagers address him as mama, a maternal uncle who was always watching out for them through good and bad times.

### Pulling a Houdini act

Tantya and the zamindars were caught in a game of catch-me-if-you-can, with Tantya and his followers robbing and looting the zamindars and government-run business establishments, which worked hand in glove with the zamindars, right under their noses. The zamindars, in turn, hatched conspiracies to trap Tantya. Caught between the two were the police, who were always late to arrive at the scene of the crime, even when they had prior information.

In November 1878, Sardar Patel lured Tantya, Bijnia and Daulia to visit Pokhar with false promises of putting past rivalries behind them and starting anew as friends. When they arrived, Tantya and his lieutenants were caught by the police and taken to Nimar to be jailed. However, the three bandits escaped from their prison cells despite heavy security.

This was followed by a false report by a zamindar that led to the capture of Daulia. As expected, he was sentenced to life imprisonment at the Jubbalpore jail. On the day the sentence was announced, the house of the said zamindar was looted and burnt, and the zamindar was murdered. The police were astounded at how it all happened under their noses. Days later, Daulia managed to escape from the Jubbalpore jail.

In 1882 alone, Tantya successfully pillaged 80 villages. By then, the police deployed detectives to trace him. Detective Inspector Ibrahim Beg reported a minor success when he nabbed a Bhil who left behind a shoe during one of the dacoities. Through him, Beg managed to come in contact with Bijnia and arrested him. Needless to say, Bijnia was sent straight to the gallows. After Bijnia's capture, Ibrahim seemed to be inching closer to nabbing Tantya when another zamindar, Khobar Patel, turned into an informant, sharing information on Tantya's whereabouts. However, this stretch of luck came to an abrupt end when Tantya rendered the family and relatives of Khobar Patel penniless.

Much like the previous instances, even in the Khobar Patel case, Tantya eluded the police and continued his banditry in the Holkar kingdom. In his signature style, he also kept escaping much before the police could arrive on the scene, leaving no clue of his whereabouts.

In the hopes of capturing Tantya and Daulia, alive or dead, the government announced cash rewards for assistance from the locals. This brought them some immediate success. A barber and a goldsmith, who also acted as spies for the British police, gave away Daulia's whereabouts, leading to his capture. But when Tantya set fire to their houses, the informants realized that their behaviour had cost them more than the reward they had earned.

### Final efforts at capture

To save the police force from the disgrace of failing to capture Tantya, Sir Lepel Griffin, agent to the Governor General in the Central Provinces, set to work along with Risaldar-Major Isri Pershad, Companion of the Indian Empire (CIE), who was part of the Central India Horse, a regular cavalry regiment of the British Indian army. Tents for watchmen on horses were pitched throughout the territory to catch Tantya whenever sighted. Despite the alertness, Tantya managed to carry out two major dacoities.

By 1887, Tantya had committed over 500 dacoities. However, his physical strength had started to wane, and, by the start of 1889, he had seriously started to consider surrendering to the government. It was with this intention that Tantya spoke to Ganpat Singh, a Rajput living in the village of Banher, in Khargone. Ganpat used to provide supplies to Tantya regularly and was aware of Risaldar-Major Isri Pershad's intention regarding Tantya. So, it was natural for Tantya to discuss the possibility of surrender with Ganpat, who, in turn, promised him that he would speak to Isri Pershad. It is not clear what transpired between Ganpat and Isri Pershad. As Deputy Commissioner of Nimar J.W. Macdougall mentioned in his letter to *The Times of India*, dated 6 October 1889, Ganpat and Isri Pershad definitely discussed the capture of Tantya, although facilitating a surrender was not their agenda.[2] Ganpat was to entice Tantya with commissioning a dacoity. However, as per Tantya's version of the story, which he shared with *The Pioneer*, Ganpat had promised Tantya a surrender.[3] Thus, Tantya visited Gapat to get more details about the surrender on the occasion of Rakshabandhan. When he reached the house, Ganpat cleverly whisked away his musket, thereby allowing the policemen who were hiding in the house to easily capture him.

### Trial, appeal and death

Tantya was brought to Jubbalpore for a trial, heavily guarded by policemen, under the directions of Assistant Superintendent of Police G.W. Gayer, lest he pull another vanishing act. On

---

[2]Mukherjee, Charu Chandra, *The Life of Tantia Bhil: The Renowned Bandit-Chief*, B.H. Dutt, Calcutta, 1890.
[3]Ibid.

28 September 1889, Deputy Commissioner Sir Stanley Ismay charged him with dacoity and mutilation. It was a long trial that lasted till 9 October. Eight witnesses gave evidence against Tantya. No one spoke in his favour. Even Jasoda identified him and denied any kind of criminal acquaintance with him. Tantya refused to cross-examine those who testified against him, as he claimed that they were all lying. At the end of this highly one-sided trial, Tantya was charged under Sections 395 and 397 of the Indian Penal Code and was sentenced to death by hanging.

Surprisingly enough, after the sentence had been pronounced, a group of lawyers of the Jubbalpore court took into account the outpouring of sympathy for Tantya in the vernacular press and sensed the unfairness of the trial. Consequently, they sent a mercy petition to the commissioner, stating that since Tantya was already on the verge of death, a death sentence did not make sense. Instead, he should be pardoned and his excellence in guerrilla warfare should be utilized by sending him to Burma, where he could assist the government in fighting the Burmese dacoits. However, this petition was declined and Tantya was hanged on 4 December 1889.

On the day of his execution, Tantya asked to be shot by soldiers and not hanged, so that he could die like a soldier rather than a common criminal. However, the deputy commissioner did not grant this last wish. After his death, his body was dumped at Patalpani, which lies along the present-day Patalpani–Kalakund rail route, about 100 kilometres away from the Khandwa railway station, which Tantya used to attack frequently. A few years later, when it was observed that trains faced an abnormal number of difficulties in proceeding beyond this point, a temple was established at the spot with wooden dolls deifying Tantya so that the driver could halt to offer his respects to the bandit—a defender of the poor, who was like an uncle to his people, and a troublemaker for the Raj. Thus, through his life, Tantya mama fulfilled the pledge that his father had made to his spiritual guru, Navgaja Pir—that he would raise his son to become a protector of the Bhil people. He would deliver them from the injustice suffered at the hands of the ruthlessly greedy moneylenders, zamindars and British officials.

# 8

## GURU GOBIND GIRI

(1858–1931)

### Massacre on a Holy Night

In 2000, Soma Parghi, a humble Bhil tribesman residing in the Khuta Tikma village in Banswara, south Rajasthan, turned 110 years old. He grew up during a terrible famine, survived a massacre, raised a family through two World Wars and fought throughout the Indian freedom struggle. Despite facing these struggles, unfortunately, the post-Independence, modern India denied Soma and his community the long-promised progress for which they had fought so hard.[1]

Soma didn't have much to show for his long life, but enough to tell as a Nath Panthi[2]—a follower of a religious sect founded by Guru Gobind Giri. He had barely entered his teens when he encountered the teachings of Gobind guruji, a fellow Bhil. The spiritual leader, in his discourses, encouraged his fellow tribesmen to live a righteous life and rise above the oppression of the rulers and the British government. That was the first time

---

[1]Mahurkar, Uday, 'Descendants of Mangad Massacare Seek Recognition for Past Tragedy', *India Today*, 30 November 1999, https://bit.ly/3HWZ0FI. Accessed on 9 March 2022.

[2]This sect was different from the Nath Panthi sect founded by the sage Gorakhnath.

in his life when young Soma felt that his life, too, had value and a purpose.

Gobind Giri's words struck a chord with many Bhil men and women as they had with Soma. They saw the quality of their lives improve as they increased their association with Gobind guruji. To them, he was no less than a messiah, so there was no way they wouldn't obey him. His call for them to raise their voice against the wrongdoings they had faced was a call from God to take action against the perpetrators of these crimes.

It was a heroic resistance that Soma, along with thousands of other Bhils aided by Guru Gobind Giri put up on that fateful full moon night of Margashirsha Purnima. Thousands died that night. Soma, though, survived, and he lived to be a part of a generation that kept alive the story of the most important fight of their lives—the attack by the British at the instigation of the native princely rulers that led to the infamous Mangarh massacre.

## The early, difficult years

Guru Gobind Giri (named Vinda at birth) was born on 20 December 1858[3] in Bedsa village in the erstwhile princely state of Dungarpur, which had accepted the supremacy of the British in 1818 along with the rest of the Rajputana states. By the time of Gobind Giri's birth, the Great Mutiny of 1857 had been crushed and the regions seized by the 'rebels' had been recaptured by the British with support from the princely states. These states had a heightened loyalty towards the British government since the country had directly come under the rule of the British Crown. This meant that taxation and revenue collection took priority over everything else, especially the

---

[3] 'Vocal for Local: Folklore of Vagad Region,' DocPlayer, https://bit.ly/3uHzaSZ. Accessed on 14 April 2022.

welfare of the people from these states.

Born into an impoverished Govalia Banjara caste of the Bhils, young Vinda did not get access to education. Instead, he accompanied his parents as they travelled to distant places selling knick-knacks to sustain their family. These business excursions fuelled the curiosity of the already inquisitive Vinda. It showed him how both the native and foreign rulers were reaping benefits by exploiting the Bhil people's poverty, illiteracy and ignorance. These circumstances led most Bhil youths to take to a life of looting and banditry, but they spiritually awakened Vinda. He spent his spare time in the company of saints, seeking to understand dharma and righteous living from them. Eventually, he became a disciple of the saint Raj Giri, who belonged to the Bundi Dashnami Panth. By the turn of the century, he had become a family man but only to lose his wife and children to the dreaded famine—the infamous Chhapniya Akaal of 1899 that had affected all of western and central India.

### Becoming Guru Gobind Giri

Upon completing his spiritual training, Vinda took on the new name of Gobind Giri and returned to Bedsa in 1908. He was unhappy to see the deplorable conditions to which the Bhils had descended. At the mercy of greedy zamindars, jagirdars and moneylenders, they worked for days with no food, water or payment, and yet, they had to pay taxes. Convinced that their lowly existence would never end and unable to bear this burden, the Bhils had taken to liquor and become morally depraved. This paved the way for the Christian missionaries to start their work among the Bhils of the Mewar Hills and Tandla. This made Gobind Giri unhappy and he saw it as an opportunity to lead the Bhils out of their misery and encourage them to live a life of dignity.

To achieve this, he set up the samp sabha,[4] a social reform movement to help the Bhils resort to ethical living and proper food habits. Gobind Giri made it his life's purpose to unite the Bhils to fight their oppressors. His first objective was to bring in a sense of social equality between the Bhils and the upper castes and ruling Rajputs. He questioned how communities, such as the Rajputs and Brahmins, who believed in the evil practices of female infanticide, sati, dowry, shunning widow remarriage and purdah, could assert themselves as being superior? To rise above such social inequalities, he set a personal example by marrying his brother's widow and adopting his nephew as his own son.

The samp sabha also advocated abstaining from meat and wine, maintaining personal hygiene by bathing daily and wearing clean clothes, always speaking the truth and not stealing or indulging in adultery. To help the Bhils lead a simple, pious and virtuous life, Gobind guruji also started the Bhagat Movement. It aimed to help the Bhils build a belief system centred around living a life of devotion to one supreme God. It also instilled faith in life after death so one would be answerable for all of one's actions during one's life. Until then, the Bhils had been living with age-old superstitious beliefs that ghosts (*virs*), witches (*vantaras*) and enchanters (*bhopas*) existed. To break such superstitions, Gobind Giri started the practice of worshipping before fire pits (*dhunis*), where they would perform havans and other rituals for self-purification. The Nath Panthis wore rosaries of rudraksh around their necks, a bandana-like yellow-coloured head gear and carried a pair of iron tongs on their person.

---

[4]'Samp' means 'unity and brotherhood'. It was a social reform movement aimed at the Bhil community to help them lead a healthier and more productive lifestyle by following a set of ten commandments.

## Seeds of reform and rebellion

When Gobind Giri first arrived in Dungarpur after completing his spiritual training, his charismatic personality and spiritual aura made him a favourite of the then ruler, Maharawal Bijeysinghji Bahadur. The Maharawal had ascended the throne during the famine of 1899 as a 10-year-old, upon the demise of his grandfather—Maharawal Shri Udaysinghji Bahadur—and had just been handed over the reins to rule. He would frequently invite Gobind Giri to the palace just to listen to his devotional singing and spiritual discourses. He also did not have any objections to the setting up of *dhunis* across the state so that the Bhils could gather for worship.

By 1912, as Gobind guruji's teachings started gaining widespread acceptance, the Bhils started gaining self-esteem, enjoying a healthy lifestyle and refusing to be victims anymore. Ever since the Bhils had embraced the commandants of the Gobind guruji, their drinking habits had reduced greatly. This led to a drop in the revenue from liquor sales. Furthermore, the Bhils started questioning their tax payments. This is when Maharawal Bijeysinghji Bahadur had a change of mind about Gobind guruji's teachings since it discomfited both the princely rulers as well as the British officials. The drop in revenue and a simultaneous unification of the Bhils rang alarm bells for the rulers of Dungarpur, Banswara, Sunth (present-day Santrampur) and Idar (in present-day Gujarat). These ruling houses were related to each other either by blood or marriage, so a threat to one automatically became a threat to the entire Rajputana ruling class. It appeared to them that the Bhils were seeking to create a state of their own. Feeling challenged, they started resenting Gobind guruji and his followers. Soon, the Nath Panthis were forbidden from gathering at their *dhunis* and practising their religion.

## Building up to an ill-fated October

In January 1913, Maharawal Bijeysinghji Bahadur of Dungarpur, who had once been fascinated by Gobind Giri, now sought to arrest and imprison him on the false charges of fleecing and deceiving the peasants. He also confiscated Gobind Giri's savings and forced him to give up his religion by imprisoning his wife and adopted son. However, fearing a severe backlash from close to five lakh Nath Panthis, Gobind Giri was released in April 1913, but exiled from Dungarpur along with his followers.

Between April and October 1913, Guru Gobind Giri and the Nath Panthis were shunted between Banswara, Idar and Sunth in search of a stable and safe place to live and worship. However, each time they found a place, officials would chase them away. Finally, extremely harassed by the Raja of Idar's attempts to capture them, the Nath Panthis, along with Gobind guruji, retired to the Mangarh Hill located along the Banswara–Sunth border in the present-day Anandpuri panchayat. Gobind Giri had set up his principle *dhuni* there a few years earlier, in 1903.[5]

Assembling in Mangarh Hill also gave the Nath Panthis an opportunity to unite publicly and unapologetically discuss their grievances. However, the wily minds of the princely rulers interpreted this action otherwise. Fearful that the Nath Panthis had taken a defensive position and were about to declare war to overthrow them and establish 'Bhil Raj', they voiced their concerns to the British political agent for the southern Rajputana states, Major R.E.A. Hamilton. In response, the agent issued a warning asking Gobind guruji and his followers to vacate the area. However, this was not to be.

The development produced a side effect. It invoked the anger of the militant faction of the Nath Panthis led by Punja

---

[5]'Massacre on ManGadh Hills', Desh-Daaz: Fierce Passion 4 Nation, 5 June 2013, https://bit.ly/3wGMo3G. Accessed on 28 March 2022.

Dhirji Parghi, the second in command of the Nath Panthis, after Gobind Giri, who did not take kindly to this warning. He did not believe that Gobind guruji's peaceful methods should be used to deal with the situation. He chose another course of action to avenge this injustice.

On 31 October 1913, accompanied by a few of his lieutenants, Dhirji attacked the police outpost at Gadra (Gadhran), near Mangarh. Apart from looting the outpost, they captured and killed Gul Mohammad, the police constable who had been sent up the Mangarh Hill to scout the area for intelligence, and took a jamadar as their prisoner.[6] The next day, his band unsuccessfully attacked Partabgarh Fort in Sunth and looted the village of Bhamri when the village headman refused to join the cause. This outing did not go to waste, as it inspired 300 Bhils from Kushalgarh, Banswara and Sunth to join Gobind Giri at Mangarh.[7] Soma Parghi was one of them.

Disturbed by this incident, on 6 November, Maharawal Shambhu Singh of Banswara, along with the Maharawal of Dungarpur, began to send their troops to beleaguer the Mangarh Hill Fort, where the Nath Panthis were residing. In response to this offensive, a delegation of the Bhils went to meet Captain J.P. Stockley, commander of Mewar Bhil Corps and Political Agent of Rewakantha C.W.M. Hudson, on 12 November for a discussion. However, both officers refused to meet the delegation. Then, on 13 November, Gobind Giri himself wrote a letter in which he presented 33 grievances of the Bhils. This included not interfering in the activities of the samp sabha, waiving taxes, abolishing forced labour and revoking the charges of sedition against Dhirji. Captain Stockley did not

---

[6] 'Full text of "The Rewakantha directory"', Internet Archive, https://bit.ly/3wGeXyg. Accessed on 28 March 2022.

[7] Vashistha, Vijay Kumar, 'The Bhil Revolt Of 1913 Under Guru Govindgiri Among The Bhils Of Southern Rajasthan And Its Impact', *Proceedings of the Indian History Congress*, Vol. 52, 1991, pp. 522–527.

respond to these demands. He merely conveyed via two village headmen—Dhirabhai and Nanjibhai—that the Nath Panthis would get freedom to pursue their religious activities and that they would be paid 1.25 rupees per plough per year. When the Bhils refused this offer, he flatly told them that they should all vacate the hill, as occupying it with arms in tow amounted to a rebellion. The Bhils didn't take heed this order either.

For the next few days, this cycle of sending warnings to vacate the hill and the Bhils ignoring them continued. The Bhils believed that it was because of the powerful presence of Gobind guruji that the British force had not attacked them yet, and assumed that this state of peace would continue. On the other hand, the princely rulers were growing increasingly worried by the minute. Finally, at 8.00 p.m. on 16 November 1913, the princely state rulers succeeded in pressuring the British commanders, Colonel Sherton, Major S. Bailey and Captain E. Stoiley to open fire on the Bhils.[8]

As the British machine guns and cannons started firing, the Bhils retaliated with whatever primitive weapons they had. But it was clear that they were outnumbered, and an unequal fight ensued that favoured the British force. Those with no means of defending themselves fled. However, in doing so, they found themselves sliding downhill to their deaths. At least 1,500 Bhils were killed and several hundreds injured.[9] A few lucky Bhils, like Soma, managed to escape unhurt. Soma's grandson recalls Soma telling him that the firing stopped early morning, when

---

[8]Nilsen, Alf Gunvald, 'Subalterns and the State in the Longue Durée: Notes from "The Rebellious Century" in the Bhil Heartland', *Journal of Contemporary Asia*, Vol. 45, No. 4, 2015, pp. 574-595. https://bit.ly/3vgbNyQ. Accessed on 14 April 2022; 'Vocal for Local: Folklore of Vagad', DocPlayer, https://bit.ly/3uHzaSZ. Accessed on 15 April 2022.

[9]Mahurkar, Uday, 'Descendants of Mangad massacre seek recognition for past tragedy', *India Today*, 30 November 1999, https://bit.ly/3HWZ0FI. Accessed on 9 March 2022.

one of the British officers saw a baby trying to suckle from its dead mother.[10] Once the firing ceased in the early hours of 17 November, Soma fled to a nearby cave along with a few others, where they hid for many days. They returned to their villages, carrying some of the dead on their shoulders, to tell the gory tale. As for Gobind Giri, he was shot in the leg and arrested along with 900 other Bhils.

## Death comes as the end

Upon his arrest, Gobind Giri, along with Punja Dhirji and several others, was imprisoned at the Ahmedabad jail. A special tribunal, led by Major Gough of the Political Department of the Government of India and Mr Allison of the Bombay Civil Services, was formed to conduct the trial, which was held on 11 February 1914. Gobind Giri was convicted under Section 121 and initially awarded a death sentence that was later reduced to ten years of rigorous imprisonment in the Hyderabad jail. However, on the grounds of good conduct, he was released in 1919, but banned from entering the Bhil strongholds of Banswara, Mewar, Dungarpur and Sirohi, which also happened to be the erstwhile princely states of present-day Gujarat and Rajasthan. Punja Dhirji was charged under Sections 121 and 302 and sentenced to life imprisonment at the Cellular Jail in the Andamans. Of the remaining Bhils, some were acquitted and others were charged under Sections 148 and 149 and made to serve three years of rigorous imprisonment.

After his release, Gobind Giri moved to Dahod in Gujarat and worked with the Bhil Seva Mandal. A few years later, he retired to Panchmahal district, where he spent his final years. Although he could not resurrect the Bhagat Movement to the same strength in the latter part of his life, he did keep the spirit

---

[10]Ibid.

# GURU GOBIND GIRI

of the Mangarh resistance alive through his song, '*O Buretia, Nahi Manu Re*' ('O White ruler, I won't give in'). It was his way of paying tribute to all the Bhil clansmen who had embraced his call to fight the injustice they had faced.

When Gobind guruji was in jail, he enjoyed great loyalty among his followers. Similarly, even though he took samadhi on 19 October 1931 at Kamboi village in the Limdi region of Gujarat, neither his teachings nor his religion have died out. As Sir Elliot Graham Colvin, the agent to the Governor General of Rajputana observed during his tour of the Rajputana states in March 1914, the Bhils had stopped drinking and committing petty crimes, choosing, instead, to pursue agriculture and live a peaceful life.[11] However, when he visited the region again in September of that year, he found that the prosecution of Gobind Giri had instilled hatred among the Bhils for the British.

To date, Soma Parghi's descendants, along with several others who lost their grandparents, great uncles and aunts, travel to Kamboi to pay their respects to Gobind guruji and have stayed in contact with his family, presently headed by his grandson Man Singh.[12]

## A lasting legacy

The Bhagat Movement awakened the Bhils politically, thereby sowing the seeds for the future revolt led by Motilal Tejawat against forced labour and the high rate of land revenue in 1921-22. Likewise, the martyrdom attained by the Bhils at

---

[11]Vashishtha, Vijay Kumar, 'The Bhil Revolt of 1913 under Guru Govindgiri among the Bhils of Southern Rajasthan and its Impact', in *Proceedings of The Indian History Congress*, pp. 522-527, Indian History Congress, https://bit.ly/36BCJ3e. Accessed on 21 March 2022.
[12]Mahurkar, Uday, 'Descendants of Mangad massacare seek recognition for past tragedy', *India Today*, 30 November 1999, https://bit.ly/3HWZ0FI. Accessed on 9 March 2022.

Mangarh didn't go in vain. In fact, just two days after the massacre, on 19 November, R.E.A Hamilton wrote to the Maharawal of Banswara regarding the need to maintain a non-intrusive approach on the socio-religious matters of the Bhils. It changed the attitude of both the princely rulers and the British government towards the Bhils. Many of these changes were implemented while Gobind guruji was still in jail. For instance, the state of Sunth granted the free use of timber for personal use to the Bhils; in Dungarpur, strict rules were framed to discourage Bhils from paying the *dapa* (bride price); while the Maharawal of Banswara encouraged his jagirdars to adopt a kind and humane approach in their interactions with the Bhils.

It is significant to note that around the same time, across the country, the concept of freedom found strong resonance in spirituality. Freedom struggles in different regions started to be regarded as movements for progress and living a virtuous life of dignity and equality. People no longer wanted to be freed from the British because that's how they had always lived. Rather, their cry for freedom had a much larger sense of purpose—they had started recognizing freedom as their birthright, and were prepared to lay down their lives for it.

# 9

## JATRA ORAON

(1894–1916)

### Fight for the Gift of God

When the First World War broke out in Europe in 1914, it caused considerable excitement among the Oraon tribe in Chota Nagpur, a land far removed from the theatre of war. This rang alarm bells among the British administrative officials. Chota Nagpur had been the working ground for the British, German and Austrian missionaries. Of the three, the German Lutherans held the strongest sway over the tribals. The Oraons broke out into songs in praise of the 'German Baba Kaiser', whose victory in the war was guaranteed, and would also free the Oraons themselves from the British. These praises were highly seditious to British ears, and the Oraons were fined, threatened or rounded up in a bid to control and stop them from propagating such activities. The British were successful in quashing this outpouring of support to a point. However, they were clueless about a movement that had been silently brewing underneath this cry for freedom in response to the greed of the moneylenders, the apathy of the zamindars and arrogance of the British government.

## The main grievance of the Oraons

The Oraon belief system centred on land being a gift from God and, therefore, it being a resource to be owned by the entire community. Though the Oraon community originated somewhere between the Gujarat and Konkan regions, through several waves of migration from the Rohtas and hills around Patna, they had settled in Chota Nagpur, a part of Bihar, by the eighteenth century. Their ancestors had carved out their land by clearing jungles and setting up villages. These initial families were the Bhumihars. They did not pay rent for this land nor did anyone dictate any terms to them. The descendants of these original settlers held privileged tenures and status over the settlers who came in later. The subsequent migrants were the Jeths and ordinary peasants, depending on how much later they arrived. The people who migrated last worked as agricultural labourers or tea garden workers in Jalpaiguri or as scavengers in Calcutta. The Tana Bhagats belonged to this group.

A *pahan* (the village priest), *pujar* (the helper) and *mahto* (village headman) were chosen from these Bhumihars. Together, these three people could access the Oraon world of spirits, conduct sacrifices and festivities, and later, negotiate between the Oraons, the zamindars and the British government. The Oraon society, thus, had its own notions of class, position, purity, pollution, prestige and status existing within the tribe that the government chose to ignore. Instead, they invaded it with their own system comprising professional moneylenders and zamindars, who were supported by the police. Adding to this was the incorrect recording of the rights and privileges under The Chota Nagpur Tenancy Act of 1908, which resulted in the registration of the wrongful ownership of land. A socio-economic conflict was, thus, apparent, and due to the presence of the Christian missionaries, it assumed the status of a religious order too. In Jatra's Tana Bhagat movement, this conflict found full expression.

## Jatra and the Tana Bhagats

This movement was founded by a 20-year-old Oraon youth named Jatra, a resident of Chingri village in Gumla, Ranchi. Jatra and his tribespeople worked as labourers who received little or no pay for the work they did, and yet, they had to pay rent and taxes. When not being employed as labourers, they acted as drum beaters or baggage carriers when the British officials went on a hunt. In 1914, the Oraons were deployed for the construction of the summer residence of Sir Charles Stuart Bayley, the first lieutenant governor of Bihar and Orissa, at Netarhat. In April that year, Jatra and a few others were asked to work as coolies at a construction site for a school located in the neighbouring village of Dokotoli. Jatra refused and so did the seven youths who were with him.

On the face of it, they should only have been reprimanded or fined for their refusal. However, the officials were unwilling to treat it as such since they were aware of the anti-establishment activities of Jatra and the youths, who had been arrested along with him.

In 1913, Jatra claimed to have had a divine vision of the Oraon deity, Dharmesh Baba. In this vision, Dharmesh Baba appointed Jatra as his messenger, told him that the Oraon race was a superior one and asked him to spread the message of simple living with devotion to God for the speedy attainment of salvation. Accordingly, Jatra assembled his tribesmen and preached to them this new concept of living a life as a Tana Bhagat, which means someone who is 'pulled by their devotion to Baba.'[1] The commandments that stemmed from this new concept demanded the Oraons to abandon the worship of spirits from the lower realms and give up alcohol and meat consumption

---

[1] Kumar, Sanjay, 'The Tana Bhagat Movement in Chota Nagpur(1914-1920)', *Proceedings of the Indian History Congress*, Vol. 69, 2008, pp. 723-731.

and singing and dancing to live the simple life of an ascetic. Soon, young Oraon men were found gathering after dinner to pray and chant invocations to drive away evil spirits. Often, these gatherings were accompanied by clapping, head-shaking and various other physical movements incomprehensible to anyone other than them. The movement gained popularity and quickly reached the districts of Palamu and Hazaribagh through messengers from Ranchi who visited the villages in these districts. Had the Tana Bhagats stuck to these villages, the British officials would not have been worried. In fact, when these activities were first reported in early 1914, the officials were quick to remark that Jatra was a 'lunatic' who needed to be placed under the observation of the civil surgeon.

What concerned them were Jatra's additions to this list of commandments—that the Oraons needed to return to shifting cultivation, not plough the fields for the zamindars or pay rent or work for free as forced labourers. Likewise, the praying and chanting, primarily meant to ward off evil spirits, now began to include the zamindars and the British, some of whom were attacked as well. This was most inconvenient for the British government because it started becoming a threat to their lives and properties, as well as a loss of revenue and manpower. So, Jatra's refusal to work actually was hinting at a larger problem waiting to strike the government.

## Capture and death

Jatra was produced before the subdivisional officer's court and charged under Section 17 of the Criminal Penal Code[2] for sedition and refusing to work for landlords and the government. It resulted in imprisonment for one and a half years. During this time, Jatra's wife Devamania directed the movement. A year

---

[2]Ibid.

later, on 2 June 1915, Jatra was released from prison. However, he did not return to his former leadership position, choosing, instead, to work on the construction of the Netarhat road in Palamau district. Though he had spent only a year in jail, Jatra's health had deteriorated due to malnutrition and the physical torture that he had suffered in prison. At the age of 22, in 1916, he died after a period of prolonged illness, suspected to be cholera.

As per his last wish, he was not cremated for seven days. During this time, Tana Bhagats from across Chota Nagpur came to pay homage to the person they had worshipped as a messiah. The occasion also served as an opportunity for the Tana Bhagats to reunite and rise against the oppression they had been facing.

However, the movement was weakened due to the lack of steady leadership after Jatra's death. Until 1921, numerous Tana Bhagats proclaimed themselves as the next messiah, Sibu Oraon being the most prominent of the lot, but none of them lasted too long.

## Merging with Gandhi's non-cooperation movement

Eventually, with the announcement of the non-cooperation movement, the Tana Bhagats found a new life. Gandhi saw the similarities between his teachings and those of the Tana Bhagats and used it as an opportunity to take them into his fold. Even before he announced the movement, he had been familiar with the situation in the region, having visited Ranchi twice in 1917 to meet Sir Edward Albert Gait, the then lieutenant governor of Bihar and Orissa. By February 1921, Gandhi's influence had grown, as evidenced by the letter from the deputy commissioner of Ranchi to the commissioner of the Chota Nagpur Division, which stated that after attending Gandhi's meeting, the Tana

Bhagats refused to pay the chaukidari taxes.[3] In response, the deputy commissioner applied the Seditious Meetings Act to stop them from attending or organizing any more of these meetings. In April 1921, the commissioner wrote to the chief secretary of the government of Bihar and Orissa, stating that the relations between the Tana Bhagats and Gandhi were getting stronger. They were participating in processions, strikes, disrupting work at courts and police stations and even spinning the charkha, all in the firm belief that soon, the British would be displaced and land would, once again, become rent-free.

The government attempted to break off the relations between the Tana Bhagats and Gandhi by employing influential citizens like the leading anthropologist S.C. Roy, barrister N.B. Aikat and other officials to talk and dissuade the Tana Bhagats from further associating with Gandhi. However, this was not to be. Dressed in khadi, wearing Gandhi caps and holding the Congress flag, many of the Tana Bhagats enrolled as Congress members by paying four annas. They attended the Congress sessions at Gaya, Belgaum, Kokanada and even Lahore. They were active participants, traveling to these places on foot, until the non-cooperation movement was abruptly called off.

## The Tana Bhagats today

Sadly, for the Tana Bhagats, the promised day hasn't arrived even today. Since Independence, they have sent letters and petitions to win back the custody of their land. For want of the original title deeds, they sent a peepal sapling from their native land to the office of the President and central government, headed by the Congress party, immediately after Independence. However, they have faced nothing but disappointments, with

---

[3]Chattoraj, A.K., 'The Tana Bhagat Movement: An Appraisal', *Proceedings of the Indian History Congress,* Vol. 60, 1999, pp. 639-644.

over 700 families whose land was auctioned off by the British still waiting for it to be restored to them and only two out of nearly 80 freedom fighters receiving pensions.[4] Despite the disappointment of not being treated justly by the Congress in post-Independence India, the Tana Bhagats continue to worship Gandhi along with Jatra Oraon. Every year, on 1 October, people gather under the statue of Jatra Oraon, modelled after his grandson Deshwa, at Chingri village. The women dress in hand-spun or synthetic khadi sarees, and the men in dhotis, Gandhi caps and janeu (the sacred thread). They chant through the night to the sound of conch shells. The next day, they place a portrait of Gandhi next to Jatra Oraon and continue their celebrations.

As of today, the Tana Bhagats are a dwindling community of around 10,000. Their faith in Jatra and Gandhi, though, remains firm as ever. However, their political allegiance has shifted from the Congress to the Bharatiya Janata Party (BJP), which reflects Gandhian principles today. This is evidenced by the octogenarian Ganga Tana Bhagat, a former Congress MLA from Mandar, who cut the century-old ties that the Tana Bhagats had with the Congress by switching over to the BJP in 2019.[5]

---

[4]Dasgupta, Sangeeta, 'Reading Adivasi Histories: Tana Bhagats in Colonial and Postcolonial Times', *Colloquium 2012-2013: "Hinterlands, Frontiers, Cities, and States: Transactions and Identities"*, Yale Macmillan Center: Program in Agrarian Studies, https://bit.ly/3Daw3pc. Accessed on 25 March 2022.
[5]Mukherjee, Sourav, 'Jharkhand: Tana Bhagat leader joins BJP, cuts century-old ties with Congress', *The Times of India*, 27 November 2019, https://bit.ly/352dHdg. Accessed on 23 March 2022.

# 10

## ALLURI SITARAMA RAJU

(1897–1924)

### The Armed Renunciant

Gam Gantam Dora and Gam Mallu Dora—two brothers belonging to the Koya tribe from the Gudem taluk of Rampa, Godavari Agency—were earnestly looking for an ascetic who had been seen around their village. Word had reached them that this renunciant could not only heal people and tame the wildest of animals but also change the course of the future. They had also heard that he had superhuman powers—he could shower arrows on wrongdoers and bullets would bounce off of his body without injuring him. They firmly believed that this holy man had all it would take to liberate the Koya tribe from the forced rule of the British.

The woes of the Koya tribals began with the introduction of the Madras Forest Act in 1882, which made it illegal for them to carry on their usual practice of shifting cultivation and took away their right to forest produce. This was done with the intention of securing high revenue from the rich forest resources of the region. Left with no means to earn a livelihood, the tribals were forced to become labourers. With the road work in Rampa in full swing, employment opportunities were aplenty. However, the corrupt forest contractors would force the tribals to either render their services for free or pay them much below the market rates. Sometimes, in the name of debt repayment, the contractors extracted free services, even from successive generations of the tribals. The tribal peasants expected their landlords, the muttadars, to protest because they, too, were impacted by the changes in succession made by the British. But, as District Magistrate C.A. Henderson of Vizagapatam had found out, the muttadars were 'trying their best to sit on the fence'.[1] Fed up with the oppression, the Koyas wanted a way out. It was around this time that they heard about the superhuman saint, and the simple-minded folks took this as a divine sign that their liberator had arrived.

The Gam brothers eventually found this holy man meditating at the temple of Lord Ram in their village and pleaded for his intervention. He responded, 'Swarajya will come, but are you ready to fight for it?' They were.

The wandering ascetic that the Gam brothers had consulted—Alluri Ramachandra Raju—was born into a Kshatriya family from the Bhimavaram taluk of the Krishna district (present-day Godavari district). His birth date is generally accepted as being 4 July 1897.[2] Fondly known as Sitarama Raju, he was the son of Venkatrama Raju, a travelling photographer, and Suryanarayanamma, a deeply religious woman. According to a report, he studied till the fourth form at the Bangarai School at Rajahmundry.[3] He didn't continue formal education beyond

---

[1]Official report dated September 9, 1922, qtd. in Atlury, Murali, 'Alluri Sitarama Raju and the Manyam Rebellion of 1922-1924', *Social Scientist*, Vol. 12, No. 4, 1984, pp. 3-33.

[2]'Alluri Sitarama Raju 125th Birth Anniversary: PM Modi Unveils 30-ft Bronze Statue of Legendary Freedom Fighter in AP', *Financial Express*, 4 July 2022, https://bit.ly/3IqKjgk. Accessed on 8 July 2022.

[3]Jamkhedkar, Arvind (ed.), *Dictionary of Martyrs: India's Freedom Struggle (1857-1947), Vol. 5*, Ministry of Culture, Government of India and Indian Council of Historical Research, 2018, https://bit.ly/364k68w. Accessed on 11 April 2022.

this point.

## Travelling across India

Instead, Raju decided to pursue his interest in Vedanta. He travelled to Benares (or Varanasi), where he spent time studying Sanskrit, astrology and palmistry. Thereafter, he is believed to have embarked on an all-India tour. Though the exact motivation behind this is not known, what we do know is that he travelled extensively across India, visiting Calcutta, Chittagong, Punjab and the Central Provinces. His travels helped him understand the true extent of the effect of colonialism across the length and breadth of the country and the movements that were countering it.

Raju fully appreciated Mahatma Gandhi's take on opposing the British style of dispensing justice and curbing the spread of liquor consumption. At the same time, he also firmly believed in the ideology of the revolutionaries. Raju's Calcutta–Chittagong outing led to him becoming a member of one of the top three secret societies of the time. These secret societies had sprung up mostly in response to the Bengal Partition and drew their inspiration from similar societies that had brought about the French, Bolshevik and Irish revolutions. These secret societies hoped to achieve the same results in India by engaging in terrorist activities, like bombing and assassination, in stark contrast to the method that Mahatma Gandhi had been preaching. Quite popular with the youth, these societies were active in both Calcutta and Dhaka, often with strong connections to newspapers and periodicals. In January 1906, the police identified 14 such clubs and societies whose activities supported the Swadeshi movement. Raju stayed in Calcutta just long enough to not attract the attention of the police and then returned to Rampa.

Back on his home ground, he could see that the Congress pracharaks had been spreading awareness about the nationalist movement. However, they hadn't been able to make the peasants understand the true meaning of the prevailing situation. Furthermore, the abrupt withdrawal of the non-cooperation movement in March 1922 left a vacuum—how exactly were the masses to protest?

### The Fituri revisited

The Fituri[4] (rebellion) wasn't new to the Koyas. They had already rebelled twice in the past against the British, starting 1839. The first phase had mostly been about the muttadars fighting to protect their independence and privileges. It was only in the second phase, which lasted between 1879 and 1880, that the tribals joined in the cause of ousting foreign rule. United by their grievances and religious beliefs, they undertook criminal activities to express their displeasure. The third time around, they were preparing to rebel under the leadership of a non-tribal leader, who they had adopted as one of their own.

When Gantam and Mallu first met Raju, the head of Gudem—their 'mutta'[5]—Virayya Dora had been jailed by the police for disobeying the law. Virayya's ancestors had been dispossessed of their right to being muttadars in the 1840s due to their involvement with the Fituri that had happened back then. Ever since, the descendants had been fighting to get back what was rightfully theirs. In early 1922, Virayya had managed to escape from prison but had been caught and put behind bars at the Rajavomangi police station. Sitarama Raju also

---

[4]The British used the word 'Fituri' rather than 'rebellion' and referred to the rebels as 'Fituris' or 'Fituridars'.
[5]Cluster of villages presided over by a person, usually appointed by the king, called muttadar.

knew that Virayya's trial had been set for 24 August 1922. As for Gantam and Mallu, their land had been confiscated by the special assistant agent[6] in 1917 and all their efforts to get back what was rightfully theirs had been futile.

Similarly, Yendu Pandal, a fellow villager and headman, had been given the contract for road construction. However, he had been refused payment upon completion of the work, citing poor construction quality. Furthermore, he was also asked to return the 100 rupees that had been given to him as an advance. Such cases of exploitation provided the perfect setting for Raju to commence his campaign against the British. He and the Koyas recruited more men from their mutta, who trained under Raju for the impending war.

## The Fituri commences

Starting 22 August, Sitarama Raju decided to consecutively attack Rajavomangi, Chintapalli and Krishnadevipeta, where he had been preaching civil disobedience and had attracted police attention. Prior to the attack, he sent out letters notifying the respective stations of his intentions. The letters were heavily dusted with chilli powder, in what can only be regarded as a message that declared, 'Dare to catch me if you can,' to the British.

In keeping with his promise, Raju began his attacks on 22 August along with an army of 500 Koya youths. After each attack, they left the police station with all the arms and ammunition they could find. Thus, by the end of the third day, on 24 August, they had amassed 26 muskets, 2,500 rounds of ammunition and several sets of police uniforms.[7] Also, they had successfully freed Virayya Dora. The Muttadar, however, felt

---

[6]Inferred to be a level below the collector and responsible for ensuring the tribals did not 'invade' the forest.
[7]Atlury, Murali, 'Alluri Sitarama Raju and the Manyam Rebellion of 1922-1924', *Social Scientist*, Vol. 12, No. 4, 1984, pp. 3-33.

no gratitude towards the Fituris, neither did he offer them any support. Carrying on with his agenda, he soon found himself recaptured by the police and was back in prison. However, the episode exalted Raju to the status of a saviour in the eyes of the Gudem public and he soon had throngs of young men joining him as Fituris.

### Efforts at scaling up

Buoyed by this success, Raju scaled up his movement. 'Don't dance attendance at the court and don't drink,'[8] was his chief bugle call. The Koyas responded by bringing down toddy shops and setting up their own local panchayat to serve justice. The open looting of and attack on three police stations with advance notice, followed by the declaration of a war of independence, took the administration by surprise. They viewed the Fituris as the coming together of dacoits, murderers, jailbirds, robbers, bandits and landless badmash to establish a new kingdom in Gudem. To deal with this, they called in the Malabar Special Police.

While the special forces were pursuing the Fituris, Raju made his way towards Kilamkota and Gangarajumadgole to recruit new fighters. They were finally intercepted on 3 September at Onjeri Ghat by Captain Kenneth Charles Tremenheere. However, despite the superiority of their equipment and weapons, the special forces suffered a humiliating defeat. Three weeks later, at the Damanapalli ghat, in the Golconda area, the Fituris ambushed a police party led by assistant superintendents of Madras Police, Scott Coward and L.N. Hayter. In response to these defeats, the government now called in the Ballary Special Forces, Coromandel and East Coast Rifles, as well as the Assam Rifles, who were trained in guerrilla warfare, to crush the Fituris.

Their efforts paid off. On 6 December 1922, a party of 100

[8]Ibid.

policemen successfully attacked the rebels in the village of Peddageddapalem. They were able to kill 12 rebels, capture six and wound several others.[9] However, the victory was short-lived. The Fituris returned twice as strong.

## Alternate tactics

Initially, the government believed Raju's attacks to be a fight for the restoration of succession rights of a few aggrieved muttadars. So, they offered him 50 acres of land, where he could build an institution of his own to serve the Koyas. However, they soon found that Raju's intentions ran much deeper, and the social base of the rebellion was the tribals. Village after village offered Raju the men and materials required for the fight. Such was their determination to fight the British that they formed their own intelligence network to spy on the police forces. The hilly terrain and the agility of the Koyas had already been proving troublesome for the police. Now, with this indigenous spy network in place, they faced the risk of getting ambushed anytime, anywhere. Also, after their December defeat, Raju had adopted a fight-and-disperse approach. This minimized the possibility of capturing a Koya during a fight.

Faced with the non-cooperation of the masses and hard-pressed for a winning strategy, the police turned to using inhumane laws to break the Fituri. Starting in 1923, a series of repressive measures began to be implemented along with the systematic disarming of the villagers. Cash awards were also announced for anyone who would provide information on the progress of the Fituri, the Gam brothers, Raju and his lieutenants, or steal their weapons. When even this failed to yield any results, the police resorted to randomly prosecuting the villagers. In February 1923, eight villagers were sentenced

[9]Ibid.

to imprisonment under the pretext of supplying incorrect information regarding the Fituri. By March 1923, the government identified the geographical base of the rebels and started exerting severe economic pressures on all the villages that fell within this geographical area, including extracting punitive taxes at gunpoint, snatching away food items from houses and imposing fines on those who weren't cooperating with the police. Nevertheless, the Fituri remained unstoppable, with Raju reaching Malkangiri in June to raise more recruits. In August, the taxes and imprisonments doubled.

### An end in sight

Fearful of the heightened repression by the British, the village munsifs (judges) and muttadars, who had supported the rebels until then, started either double-timing or backtracking on their support. This eventually opened up the possibility of capturing Raju and crushing the uprising. Finally, on 18 September, Gantam Dora was captured from Nadimpalem village. News of his presence at this village was passed on to the police by three of the village munsifs on conditions of anonymity. Further, they also requested that their rewards be paid after the Fituri had ended, so that they didn't appear as traitors.

Losing one of his trusted lieutenants was hard for Raju. However, he braved this ordeal. In September 1923, he advanced to Paderu, in present-day Vishakhapatnam. In January 1924, a unit of the Assam Rifles was deployed to intensify patrolling in the area. Ultimately Raju was trapped by the patrol force in the forests of Chintapalli and captured on 6 May 1924. The next day, in the village of Koyyuru, he was tied to a tree and shot dead. His body was brought to Krishnadevipeta, tied to a cot in a standing position and buried on 8 May 1924.

Over the next two months, the government ended the Fituri by capturing 186 villages and 276 Koya youths, who were active participants in the uprising. Most were sentenced to life imprisonment. Mallu Dora was one of them. After India gained Independence, he was elected as a Lok Sabha member in 1952. The rest were charged with supplying false information to the police. As a result, their property was confiscated, and they were sentenced to two years of imprisonment and a fine of 1,000 rupees was imposed.

## A change of stance

So long as Sitarama Raju was alive and fighting fervently against the colonial forces, he received little recognition from the prominent leaders of the time and even received unfavourable attention from the press. In April 1922, after the Chauri Chaura incident, Raju was interviewed by the *Andhra Patrika*. In this interview, he expressed his disappointment with Mahatma Gandhi calling off the non-cooperation movement. The paper supported his ideology by asking for a detailed investigation into the issues raised by the tribals of the region. Other regional journals like *Kisan Patrika*, along with the Congress, had openly sided with the British, asking for more forces to be deployed to crush the rebellion.

However, post his martyrdom, *Kisan Patrika* and the Congress were quick to elevate him to the likes of Vladimir Lenin, Shivaji Maharaj, Maharana Pratap and George Washington. Conversely, *Andhra Patrika* pointed out the futility of adopting a violence-based method to gain Independence. Mahatma Gandhi, while disapproving of the armed approach of the movement, paid tribute to Raju's bravery and sacrifice.

The Rampa rebellion remained localized mainly due to the unwillingness of political parties to align forces with it and its desertion by the Congress. However, it successfully lit the fire of patriotism in the nearby Malkangiri and the state of Jeypore, as leaders of this region geared up for the next phase of the freedom struggle.

# 11

## LAXMAN NAYAK

(1899–1943)

### The Man Who Brought Quit India to Odisha

The tiny town of Mathili, situated along the Jeypore-Malkangiri road, and an administrative block headquarters of Malkangiri district in Odisha, is home to the Bonda tribe. Apart from a police station, school and dispensary, Mathili, then part of the Koraput district, had nothing much to offer to its residents, numbering just a little over a thousand. Yet, at the crack of dawn on 21 August 1942, there was palpable excitement in the air. Over the last few days, Mathili had welcomed a steady stream of people from the nearby villages. They had also been listening to the frequent lectures of the mustadar, or village headman, of Tentuliguma—Laxman Nayak. Nayak had been urging the tribesmen to resist the British officials for their very presence and their policies that had robbed them of their freedom, land and earnings. The tribesmen were convinced they had to do or die for their motherland. The atmosphere was perfectly suited for the plan ahead.

At 9.30 a.m., thousands of tribesmen from in and around Mathili marched towards the police station, each carrying a Congress flag. They were chanting the 'Ramdhun' with intermittent shouts of 'Swaraj has come!', 'The British government is gone!', 'The old Raja of Jeypore is dead!', 'Mahatma Gandhi ki jai!' Their goal was to hoist the Congress flag on top of the police station, which would eventually lead to their court arrest. 'We will not raise a hand, even if we are beaten,' Laxman had briefed them. The marching crowd was unceremoniously intercepted by a small force of police patrollers halfway through, at the marketplace, and ordered to disperse. In response, the demonstrators waited for about an hour and proceeded to the police station. This time, Mujibur Rahman, the magistrate on duty, ordered a lathi charge and violence erupted.

As the demonstrators broke down the bamboo fence surrounding the station and forced their way in, the policemen beat them up mercilessly. When there was no sign of the situation improving, the police opened fire. Two of the protestors, Nakul Madkami and Linga Bhumia, nearly succeeded in hoisting the flag but were shot dead. Everyone present was injured, though only 17 were critically injured and five died. Laxman was one of the seven who were beaten severely. In fact, thinking that he was dead, he was thrown into a nearby ditch. Hours later, Laxman gained consciousness and, with great difficulty, made his way to Jeypore to meet his fellow Congress worker Balbhadra Pujari, who advised him to move back to his village Tentuliguma.

Born on 22 November 1899, into a family belonging to the Bhuyan tribe, Laxman inherited the title of mustadar from his father Padlam Nayak in 1930 when he was 31. A musta was a group of villages headed by a person of authority—the mustadar. This appointment was usually made by the king and was hereditary in nature. Even though Malkangiri had been integrated into the Madras Presidency, it had come under the Jeypore zamindari after the Madras Permanent Settlement Regulation had been introduced in 1802. Some time after that, it had been leased out to the last queen of Malkangiri, Bangara

Devi, but in 1872, the Maharaja of Jeypore took it over for a sum of 3,500 rupees and brought it directly under his control.[1] The mustadari system continued.

Growing up, Laxman understood that though being a mustadar sounded like being a representative of the king, in essence, he owned the land jointly with nearly all of his relatives. Laxman had 90 relatives and the total land shared between them was about 70 acres. Bonded labourers who served for a few years to pay off a debt, agricultural labourers who were paid one and a half *kunchams* (a measure of grain) of paddy per day, daily wage coolies who charged 3-4 annas a day, settled agriculturists and the shifting cultivators worked on the land. The mustadars received rent from the agriculturists and cultivators based on the production capacity of the land and the number of ploughs and hoes they owned. Based on this rent, the mustadars paid a tax to the king.[2]

## A disruptive British presence

With the arrival of the British on the scene, the existing situation got complicated. Firstly, the British demoted Jeypore to a zamindari estate. Subsequently, they introduced the Madras Estates Land Act in 1908, under which only the British government had the right to the forest, and its produce and *podu* or shifting cultivation was banned. Overnight, the masses lost their livelihood, and the mustadars found themselves at the mercy of outsiders. Tax rates were inconsistent and hereditary rights could be taken away randomly. It was an unpleasant situation for everyone.

---

[1]Behuria, N. C., *Final Report on the Major Settlement Operations in Koraput District 1938-64*, Orissa Govt. Press, Cuttack, 1966.
[2]Pati, Biswamoy, 'Storm Over Malkangiri: A Preliminary Note On Laxman Naiko's Revolt (1942)', *Proceedings of the Indian History Congress*, Vol. 41, 1980, pp. 706-721.

Malkangiri was not new to revolting against the injustice meted out to its people by the British government. The Koya revolt of 1879-80, led by Tammanna Dora, had impacted the southern region of Malkangiri positively by uniting the suffering masses to rise against the British atrocities. In fact, Tammanna Dora had not only found refuge in Malkangiri after escaping the British police from Rampa in Vishakhapatnam but had also been hailed as the new raja of Malkangiri. However, during the Rampa rebellion of 1922-24, led by Alluri Sitarama Raju, the Maharaja of Jeypore had offered support to crush the rebellion. Laxman was already aware of the difficulties he was facing as a mustadar, and his proximity to the people due to the nature of mustadari system, made him understand their problems as well. Given his unique position, he could choose between the rules laid out before him without questioning them, or he could go with the flow of revolting against the political situation prevalent at that time. He chose the latter. Sitarama Raju's personality and approach to outwitting the British deeply impacted Laxman and was instrumental in shaping the latent freedom fighter in him.

Like Raju, Laxman too developed an interest in astrology and medicine. He was also able to befriend Ramchandra Kutia, a Koya youth, who had been part of Raju's Fituri (rebellion), and learnt how to use a gun from Kutia.

Many of Laxman's fellow mustadars were Congress workers and so were many of his relatives. On 1 April 1936, Koraput and the coastal districts of Ganjam, Balasore, Puri, Cuttack and Angul were designated as the new Orissa Province of British India and the Congress began to assert its presence in the area by establishing a Provincial Congress Committee in it, which served as a revolutionary governmental structure that raised manpower and funds to organize the movement against the British rule along with deciding the bill of rights for the state. In 1936, Laxman had the opportunity to attend the Congress meeting that was held at Malkangiri. Shortly thereafter, he enrolled as a 'four anna member'[3] of the Congress at its party office in the Nuaput village. In the party office, he systematically understood what nationalism meant and what national integration stood for. One of the many activities that he undertook at this point was organizing the masses to protest against the age-old practice of bonded labour. It was mostly the tribals who had been victims of this practice. Hence, Laxman's initiative of opposing bonded labour by encouraging people to disobey the moneylenders and British officials when they were forced to serve without due payment was well-supported across his musta. This initiative helped the Congress win three seats in the ensuing legislative election of 1937. The Congress candidates—Radhakrushna Biswas Ray, Radhamohan Sahu and Sadashiv Tripathy—won against zamindars and members of the Maharaja's family. With this win, both Laxman and the Congress came to be regarded as synonymous with each other.

## Gearing up for revolt

Congress meetings were now being conducted at various places throughout the district with increasing frequency and people were becoming members of the Congress in large numbers. In 1938, a three-month-long training camp was held at Nuaput, where around 400 new members were trained in khadi spinning, scouting and village service, including farming, animal husbandry and liquor prohibition. Needless to say, Laxman played a key role in all these activities.

By 1939, he ensured that the charkha found its way to the most remote corner of Malkangiri, the tribals gave up hunting and meat-eating, and ashram schools were established in every

---

[3]The 'four anna membership' was launched at the Nagpur session of the Congress in 1920 to enable more poor people to join the party.

village. Consequently, the party membership rose to around 56,000. Tentuliguma, Laxman's ancestral village alone, boasted of 200 members. In the same year, Laxman led the 'No Rent Payment' campaign in Mathili and was promptly arrested for it. This was just the beginning of a series of protests that would be carried out by the future martyr. In 1940–41, as part of the civil disobedience movement, Laxman conducted extensive meetings, discussions and sloganeering against taxation, *bethi* (the provision of labour service without payment), *goti* (unpaid bonded labour), and *gudem* (the supply of free food, drinks and rest houses to visiting government officials and employees of the zamindar). This also led him to individual satyagraha twice—first at Ramgiri and second at the Mathili police station. Both times, he was sentenced to rigorous imprisonment of six months and had to pay a fine of 300 rupees.

Laxman's activities turned him into a mass hero, but this popularity was worrisome for the Maharaja of Jeypore, who had allied with the British administration. Together, they kept trying to instigate opportunist moneylenders, thugs and other mustadars against Laxman. However, they weren't successful.

On 31 July 1942, Laxman attended the last meeting of the Congress at Jeypore where the Quit India resolution was reaffirmed and instructions given to various district leaders to carry out the resolution. Radhakrushna Biswas Ray was sent to Bombay to attend the All India Congress Committee session and receive detailed plans for Koraput. However, he was detained in Bombay along with Sadashiv Tripathy on 9 August.

As part of the movement, the Congress leaders decided to observe hartals, not pay taxes, make salt and disrupt the functioning of government offices and police stations. In Koraput, the message was translated into the tribal language and sent out. It had an instantaneous effect as hartals and arson broke out spontaneously. All the leaders of the movement, except for Laxman, were taken into custody. Yet, the protests continued. Shops were looted, wholesale depots raided, records of the excise depot set on fire, entrances to police stations blocked and the Jeypore taluk office gheraoed. On 17 August, Laxman, along with Balaram Pujari, a fellow Congress worker, mobilized a group of 200 people and attacked liquor shops at Kongrabeda, Chandrabeda and Kuntipalli, as this affected the revenue of the administration. The next day, they were smashing wine containers at Sindhadeba.[4]

### 'Mother India shall be independent!'

In the meantime, Laxman received the plan for the satyagraha demonstration due on 21 August 1942. He immediately briefed the villagers and gathered a committed set of people to organize a peaceful protest march to the Mathili police station to hoist the Congress flag. However, the event turned out to be anything but peaceful. The police mercilessly beat Laxman, set fire to his moustache and dragged him along the rough grounds before dumping him inside a pit. In the ensuing lathicharge and firing, one of the many who died was a forest guard, G. Ramayya. An opium addict, he had, unfortunately, wandered into the midst of the violent mob and was killed. The British and the estate authorities saw this as a fantastic opportunity to frame Laxman for Ramayya's death and get him out of their way once and for all.[5]

As Laxman escaped to Tentuliguma through the forest, the police issued an arrest warrant, naming him as the accused in the murder of G. Ramayya. An intensive manhunt was launched, and on 2 September, Laxman and Balaram Pujari were arrested from their village. He was first taken to the Mathili police station,

---

[4]Pati, Biswamoy, 'Storm Over Malkangiri: A Preliminary Note On Laxman Naiko's Revolt (1942)', *Proceedings of the Indian History Congress*, Vol. 41, 1980, pp. 706–721.
[5]Ibid.

where they were tortured by the police before being presented before the court of the Deputy Magistrate Somanath Mishra, who pronounced them guilty and transferred the case to the sessions court.

On 18 September, they were sent to the Koraput jail and tried at the additional sessions court. The government charged Laxman and Balaram with arson, rioting and murder. Although the arrested duo stated that these were baseless accusations, the judge, V. Ramanathan, was convinced by the prosecution's case. Accordingly, after two months of the hearing, on 13 November 1942, V. Ramanathan read out the judgment that declared Laxman as the murderer of G. Ramayya under Section 302 of the Indian Penal Code and sentenced him to death by hanging. Balaram Pujari was sentenced to life imprisonment, with the first nine years meant to be rigorous imprisonment.

As convict number 661, Laxman was moved to the Berhampur jail on 16 November, joining Biswas Ray, Tripathy and Sahu, who were already jailed there. Though Laxman's execution was imminent, Laxman filed an appeal through a Berhampur advocate, Radha Charan Das, at the Patna High Court. However, the appeal was rejected, and on 13 January 1943, the sentence was reconfirmed, and the execution date was set for 4.00 a.m. on 29 March of the same year. As news of the confirmation of his execution spread, there was grief and anger among the masses.

To his family, Laxman offered consolation and asked his brother-in-law, Bansing Pujari, to look after them. To his fellow freedom fighters, he offered encouragement. On the eve of his hanging, Laxman requested that he be allowed to meet with Biswas Ray, Tripathy and Sahu. Only Tripathy could meet him. In this last conversation, Laxman confided that his only regret was not being able to see the country gain independence.

That night, the wards were checked for any hidden weapons and then firmly locked. Fellow prisoners prayed and wept through the night. A sense of helplessness at not being able to save Laxman from the gallows filled the air. As the scheduled hour drew closer, Laxman, with his head covered under a long black cap and hands tied behind him, walked out of his cell towards the gallows, amid the chants of 'Inquilab Zindabad' by the inmates. On approaching the gallows, Laxman spoke his final words to the hangman, Ramamurthy Rao, who, in this case, was the jailer as well, 'If the sun is true and so is the moon, then it is equally true that Mother India shall be independent!' The hangman complied with his duties, an act for which he received 25 or 30 rupees, a bottle of wine and a day off.[6]

The Quit India movement at Mathili certainly shook the British government. They punished the masses by levying heavy fines, terrorizing people and forcing them to sell their land. As a result, the movement gradually subsided. As for the Congress, it began to get steadily pressurized by popular forces such as the Jeypore estate authorities and the British government. In order to strengthen itself, the Congress realized that it would have to partially realign itself, so it beat a momentary retreat.

---

[6]Nayak, Birendra, 'Hanging of Laxman Naik: A Tribal Gandhite', *The Tribal Tribune*, https://bit.ly/3xpxhMv. Accessed on 14 April 2022.

# 12

## KOMARAM BHEEM

(1900–1940)

### A Small Rebellion with a Big Fallout

Komaram Bheem was 15 years old when his mother died. Her sudden passing came as a shock. However, Bheem saw it as her being released from the cruel circumstances of her life. A year earlier, along with her son and other villagers, she had the misfortune of watching her husband, Chinnu, being slaughtered by the Razakars, the Nizam of Hyderabad's army, when he refused to pay them a bribe and thwarted their illegal attempts to snatch the land that his family owned. There wasn't much for her to live for after that.

It was a different matter for Bheem. Like his forefathers, Bheem knew that for his forest-dwelling community, life centred on forests. If anyone had any right to the forests, it was his people—the Gonds—not the zamindars, forest guards, patwaris or the junglaat police (forest police). For that matter, not even the ruler who, in this case, was the Nizam of Hyderabad. So, it would be unfair to allow these alien forces to confiscate what rightfully belonged to the Gonds. Someone had to put a stop to the events that had been unfolding for some time. Bheem's father had done so and paid the price for it. Now, it was for Bheem to continue this quest.

## An uneasy childhood

Bheem was born on 22 October 1900 into the Gond (Koitur) community at Sankepalli village near Asifabad, a region near present-day Adilabad that shares its border with the Yavatmal and Chandrapur districts of Maharashtra.[1] His childhood was spent migrating from one place to another, as his community practised *podu* cultivation. Growing up, he watched his village elders suffer humiliating punishments meted out by the junglaat police for failing to pay *Dupapetti*—the tax for collecting firewood and *Bambram*, the tax on cattle grazing. The forest police were usually recruited by the moneylenders and zamindars to extract money from the tribals by threatening their lives and properties. Occasionally, they accepted bribes from the tribals, but mostly, this was only a temporary relief, as they wasted no time in returning with bigger demands.

After the Indian Forest Act was introduced in 1865, it became increasingly difficult for the Gonds to find land to graze their cattle, cultivate their crops and find firewood. The Act categorized the forests into reserved, protected and village forests. This meant that communities like the Gonds, who lived on forest produce and cultivated the land, could no longer do so. They had already lost their right to teak when Lord Dalhousie declared it as the State's property in 1855. With their essential survival mechanisms gone, how were they going to pay any tax? It wasn't as if the rulers or administration had offered them an alternate mode of employment or compensated them. Instead, they were victimized through various forms of bonded labour like *bhagela*, *begari* and *vetti*, where mostly the tribals were hired to do strenuous work at minimal or no cost.

---

[1]Kumar, Ramnaresh, 'Komaram Bheem—the Man Who Led the Tribal Revolt against Hyderabad's Nizam', Dakshināvarta, 29 October 2020, https://bit.ly/3JPJrBt. Accessed on 28 March 2022. Komaram Bheem's year of birth is contested to be either 1900 or 1901. We believe it is 1900.

## Caught between the British and the Nizam

Even without the Forest Act, the Gonds and the British shared an uncomfortable relationship. This was a community that had previously been ruled by the Gond kings of Chandrapur. However, when the kingdom was annexed by the British in Nagpore due to the long-drawn rebellion by various Gond kings, primarily Ramji Gond and Baburao Shedmake, the Gonds escaped to the forests while the British sought to destroy and plunder them to assert their power. The British administration became suspicious of the Gond community as a whole. So, they encouraged the native princely rulers, in this case the Nizam of Hyderabad, to tighten their vigilance of the Gonds.

Uneducated, unemployed and constantly fighting to survive, Bheem led a life of isolation, much like the rest of the Gond community. It had not made any difference to him that Hyderabad had gotten a new Nizam when 25-year-old Mir Osman Ali Khan, Asaf Jahi VII, ascended the throne on 29 August 1911. Mir Osman Ali Khan's focus was to modernize the state. However, in doing so, he overlooked the pre-existing feudal structure in his administrative system, which led to his disconnect from the troubles faced by the tribals. Thus, he unwittingly ended up encouraging a part of his private militia, the Razakar army, into silencing them without giving them a chance at justice.

This rogue faction of the Razakar army joined hands with the junglaat police leading to numerous instances where the Razakars stormed into the makeshift houses of the Gonds, challenged their right to land and cattle and demanded fines or bribes. If they couldn't pay up, the Razakars would cut off their fingers.

It was during one such incident involving Bheem and his brother that Bheem killed one of the Razakars. This was the first time the Gonds of the region had fought back against the zamindars. It would only be a matter of time before a unit of the Nizam's state police would be dispatched to hunt him down. Fearing for his life, Bheem first escaped to Chandrapur and went to Pune from there.

## A resurrected Bheem

Bheem's exile proved to be life-changing. For the first time, he came in contact with the world outside his native land. He heard about similar misfortunes of Gonds elsewhere and the exploits of Ramji Gond, Baburao Shedmake and Alluri Sitarama Raju. These leaders inspired Bheem, and he decided to work towards uniting the Gonds to ask them to fight for their right to their forest land and to protest against their exploitation through lifelong unpaid labour. It is also believed that he learnt to read and write during this period. In 1937, with this newfound inspiration and strength, Bheem returned to Asifabad but chose to settle down in Babejhari village, which came under the jurisdiction of the Dhanora State Forest.

The chief grievance of the Gonds was that while the non-tribals could get a patta, a written document stating their ownership of a piece of land, they couldn't. On the contrary, they saw their own land being given away to non-tribals. They resented this deeply. All was going well for the residents of Babejhari until one day, it was announced that anyone who did not own a patta would have to vacate the land by a set date. On the announced date, the Gonds without a patta had still not left the village. In response to this, the junglaat police burnt down their houses. Upon complaining to the concerned revenue inspector and zamindar, Bheem's family, along with nine others, were allotted some land at Jodheghat, a few miles east of Babejhari.

For a while, everything was peaceful. Then, the demands of the junglaat police resumed. This time, they demanded a bribe of 500 rupees in return for the permission to continue tilling the forest lands. This money was somehow collected and paid. But soon, the guard was back, this time asking for an additional 2,000 rupees, which would have to be paid to the forest ranger.[2] At this, Bheem decided to directly report the matter to the officials of the forest department in Hyderabad.

This trip that Bheem undertook with four others is believed to have been a successful one, as they returned with permission from the officials to cultivate 57 acres of land at Jodheghat. The forest guard still insisted on the payment. When Bheem made it clear that no more such payments would be made, the guard threatened to serve them the same way they had been treated at Babejhari.

## The battle of Jodheghat

Bheem was intelligent, and even though he regarded Sitarama Raju as his hero, he didn't want to start an armed rebellion immediately. He wanted to find a peaceful solution through mediation. Nevertheless, he had secretly trained a group of Gond youths in warfare so that they could fight, if the need arose.

After the forest guard issued his threat, Bheem sent a petition by registered post to the divisional forest officer and a copy to the talukdar (the subcollector). In this petition, he once again requested permission to stay and pursue cultivation at Jodheghat. Unfortunately for Bheem, even before the petition could reach its destination, the forest guard returned with the ranger and several other guards, including an Arab trained in shooting a gun.

On reaching Jodheghat, they first burnt down several cattle sheds, and the Arab shot Bheem through his hand. The enraged

---

[2]von Fürer-Haimendorf, Christoph, Elizabeth von Fürer-Haimendorf, *The Gonds of Andhra Pradesh: Tradition and Change in an Indian Tribe*, Routledge, 1979.

ns rounded up the guards and beat them up before letting them go. Though the Gonds did not raise arms against the guards, under the leadership of Bheem, they did something far more audacious—they sent a letter to the Nizam demanding separate statehood for Gonds and the release of all those from their community who had been jailed under false accusations.

## A failed negotiation

The Nizam ordered the collector of Asifabad, Abdul Sattar, to discuss the matter with Bheem and come up with a mutually amicable solution. However, the collector had other ideas. He wanted Bheem to surrender instead. Twice, the emissaries sent by Abdul Sattar failed in their mission. The third time, Abdul decided to go in person. Before doing so, he sent word to Bheem that either he should surrender or be prepared to die at the hands of the collector. He received no reply.

Early on the morning of 1 September 1940, which happened to be the auspicious occasion of Ashwayuja Purnima, Abdul Sattar reached Jodheghat with a unit of armed policemen. They were spotted at a distance by women who were on their way to the well to collect drinking water. To avoid raising the alarm unnecessarily, a few of them quickly dispersed and went to Bheem's residence as well as the residences of his close aides to inform them of Abdul Sattar's presence in the village.

By the time Abdul Sattar and his police party arrived, Bheem and his mini army were ready for a fight. Abdul Sattar stayed true to his words—when Bheem refused to surrender, he opened fire. With this began a short but intense battle which was unequal in terms of the weapons used. Eventually, the Gond guerrilla warfare was subjugated by the collector's policemen. Bheem was killed, along with fifteen others. Their bodies were riddled with bullets until they became unrecognizable and then hurriedly burnt, so as to eliminate all physical trace of their existence.

## The aftermath

Maru and Bhadu, two of Bheem's aides who survived the attack, later recounted the brave and intelligent fight put up by Bheem. After his martyrdom, Maru and Bhadu kept up his mission and fighting spirit to ensure that their demands were met. Though Bheem's rebellion was short-lived during his own lifetime, it continued for many years after his death, ultimately merging with the Communist-led Telangana Rebellion of 1946–51 against the Nizam. Subsequently, his efforts were pushed into near oblivion. It was only in 2016, two years after the formation of the state of Telangana, that the district of Asifabad was renamed Komaram Bheem Asifabad Zilla, thus reminding the Gonds of their ultimate goal.

Today, the situation of Komaram Bheem's descendants is far from improving. The granddaughter of the martyr, Jangubai, works as a cook in a hostel, earning barely ₹3,000 a month, struggling to cultivate her one acre of land, repaying a crop loan of ₹15,000 and aspiring for an LPG connection.[3]

---

[3]Kumar, Dinesh, 'Telangana Assembly Elections 2018: Kumaram Bheem's Granddaughter Works as Cook at School', *The Times of India*, 30 November 2018, https://bit.ly/3CYM3un. Accessed on 21 March 2022.

# 13

## HELEN LEPCHA

### (1902–1980)

## The White Orchid Braveheart

The year was 1940 and 38-year-old Sabitri Devi (née Helen Lepcha) had just finished writing a letter. Glancing around cautiously, she stuffed the piece of paper inside the freshly baked bread that had come from her husband's bakery. The bread had to be delivered to a certain house at Giddepahar, near Kurseong in present-day West Bengal. She summoned a brave, loyal little boy from her neighbourhood for this. Handing over the parcel to the boy, she carefully reminded him to wait for the envelope that he would be given in return for the bread. He was to bring it to her without attracting any attention to himself. Assuring her of a safe delivery, the boy left and Sabitri Devi returned to her seat by the window and continued stitching a male Pathan dress. She had already arranged for the beard and moustache that was to accompany the get-up.[1]

---

[1] Molommu, Shera Pandi, 'Helen Lepcha Alias Sabitri Devi: Lone Freedom Fighter From the Lepcha Tribe', *International Journal of Informative & Futuristic Research*, Vol. 2, No. 9, 2015, pp. 3242–3246, https://bit.ly/3Dbx1BJ. Accessed on 25 March 2022.

A year after this incident, Netaji Subhas Chandra Bose escaped from India into the tribal territories of Kabul. That he had managed to do so despite being under house arrest was remarkable. Sabitri Devi played a central role in his escape. The determination, focus and perseverance that Sabitri Devi displayed in this sensational and historic incident was merely an extension of her quiet but strong personality. It was to become her trademark for life.

## In Kurseong, the land of the white orchid

Helen was born in 1902 to Achung Lepcha and his wife, a humble farmer-couple living in the remote village of Sangmu in Namchi, South Sikkim. In 1906, Achung Lepcha came to Kurseong along with his wife and seven daughters in search of better employment and quality of life. In 1905, Bengal was partitioned by Lord Curzon, the then viceroy of India, making the country go up in flames of protest. In this scenario, Kurseong, along with Kalimpong and Darjeeling, was fast becoming a hotspot for the Swadeshi movement led by the Indian National Congress in response to the Partition.

A sparsely populated town until the 1830s with barely two or three families from the Lepcha community, Kurseong had largely been a Bhutanese locality. Kurseong and Kalimpong came under British rule in 1865, as part of the Treaty of Sinchula signed in the aftermath of the Anglo-Bhutanese or Duar Wars fought between Bhutan and British India. Along with these territories, Bhutan also had to cede the trade routes leading into Assam and Bengal, in return for an annual subsidy of 50,000 rupees. Together with Darjeeling, Kurseong and Kalimpong were much-sought-after hill stations that offered an escape from the Indian summer. Also, since General George William Aylmer Lloyd's visit in February 1829, Kurseong had been identified as altitudinally well-suited for a much-required sanatorium and evaluated to be highly beneficial for the Company to keep an eye on the trade routes with Tibet. Since then, Kurseong emerged as a hub of social and economic development due to the trade marts opened with Tibet, the bazaars, tea gardens, coffee plantations and orchards laden with European fruits, all of which catered to an established settlement of around seventy European families. The missionaries, led by Rev. William Macfarlane—the first Scottish missionary to visit Darjeeling in 1870 to focus on vernacular education—also contributed to the growth of the region by setting up a network of primary schools, a vocational training institute and a school-cum-orphanage for Eurasian destitutes, while the presence of the sanatorium, jail and British soldiers added quintessential drama to everyday life.

The Lepcha family tried to make sure they led a normal life, even if times were turbulent with severe political unrest. Four-year-old Helen went to a local school with her siblings. At school, she heard teachers talking about jailed Congress leaders. She witnessed the burning of British-made goods on the streets, while her parents would discuss the progress of the movement at home. Even leisure time was coloured with patriotic sentiments—everyone would sing folk songs composed by the plantation labourers about overcoming oppression and being free of the British sahibs.

## A matter of choice

Growing up, Helen had two clear choices before her: one that would allow her to enjoy the newly evolved fast life of Kurseong, the hill station; the other which would mean treading the fiery path of the freedom struggle that could lead to having to give up basic comforts and face jail time or even death. Luckily for her, the commencement of the First World War in 1914 lifted the veil off the long-promoted belief that Western civilization was superior, advanced and to be desired. Instead, the fact that spinning, weaving and selling khadi could lead to economic independence found favour in her young mind.

The 14-year-old Helen found herself drawn to this bigger cause of freedom from the British, like many of her school-going friends. In 1916, after attending a Congress meeting in Kurseong, headed by Dal Bahadur Giri—the Darjeeling head of the Congress party—Helen became one of the first from her community to join the party, and, consequently, the freedom struggle. Quitting school, she joined the Khadi Movement started by Mahatma Gandhi. In 1918, she went to Calcutta, where her elder sister lived, and enrolled at the charkha training school run by Motimala Devi, the granddaughter of Pandit Ishwar Chandra Vidyasagar. Her dedication and deft skills at charkha-spinning and khadi-weaving impressed her instructors and in 1927, she was chosen to represent Calcutta at the national-level Khadi and Charkha Exhibition in Muzaffarpur in Bihar in 1927.

During the Bihar floods of 1920, Helen volunteered to do relief work and was praised for her selfless contribution. When Mahatma Gandhi came to tour the flood-affected region, he heard about Helen's work from Safidat, a leading Congress leader of the area. A meeting was arranged between Mahatma Gandhi and Helen. Impressed by her work and personality, he invited her to Sabarmati Ashram. It was during her stay at the Sabarmati Ashram that Helen deepened her understanding of the Gandhian philosophy of non-violence and satyagraha in order to lead a meaningful life. At the suggestion of Mahatma Gandhi, Helen changed her name to Sabitri Devi.

### A powerful woman in politics

This was the time when women leaders of the Congress, like Sister Nivedita, Madam Bhikaiji Cama, Annie Besant and Sarojini Naidu, among many others, were spreading the fire of Indian nationalism, both in India and abroad. Getting to hear them and working closely by their side strengthened Sabitri's resolve. Soon, she was assigned the responsibility of leading the masses in Patna, Danapur, Bakipur, Muzaffarpur and the Jharia coalfields. Working with dedication, she soon proved herself to be a capable and influential leader. Her anti-British activities soon brought her under their scanner. She became one of the most wanted Congress leaders from the Bihar and Uttar Pradesh region. A warrant was issued against her and intelligence officers were deployed round the clock to keep track of her movements and activities. Once, when she was leading a horseback rally, she was shot at by the British. Luckily, the bullet missed her. But none of this shook her spirit.

In 1919, the Jallianwala Bagh massacre took place in Amritsar, Punjab, exposing the brutal face of the British Raj. The incident killed nearly 379 and wounded over 1,200, 192 of whom were severely injured. The brutality of the incident led to the patriotic fervour in the country reaching its peak. Mahatma Gandhi reinforced this fervour by launching the non-cooperation movement in 1921. People started returning their government titles, shunning schools, rejecting foreign goods and refusing to pay taxes.

Sabitri Devi initiated her contribution towards the non-cooperation movement by leading a rally of thousands of labourers at the Jharia coalfields as she held the Indian national flag in her hand. However, she had to return to Kurseong to care for her ailing mother. Despite this personal challenge, she successfully launched a door-to-door campaign asking families to boycott foreign goods in Kurseong and Siliguri. Furthermore, she led marches that collected British goods and burnt them in huge bonfires, even when the government had imposed Section 144 to prohibit such gatherings. Failing to control her movement and that of the participating masses, the police resorted to a lathicharge. On 30 January 1922, it was evident that the police actions had been ineffective. So, they opened fire and eventually took Sabitri Devi into custody along with the Congress secretary and several other Gorkha volunteers. An anti-government case was registered against her and she was sentenced to three months of imprisonment at the Darjeeling Sadar jail. After her release, she was put under house arrest and was not allowed to move out of Kurseong for three years. When Sabitri Devi's house arrest was lifted, she immediately went back to serving her people and country. Under the guidance of leaders from the Congress Mahila Samiti, she formed groups of women that worked for the health, hygiene and education of women and children. Her dedication and popularity made her the first woman commissioner of the Kurseong municipality.

### The role women played

It was only in the 1930s that women, especially students, began to actively participate in the Indian freedom struggle in an unprecedented manner. They were involved both actively and passively, depending on whether they were students, wives, mothers or unmarried women and they were equally fierce in their fight, be it in the non-violent or revolutionary methods deployed against the British. For all of them, Sabitri Devi served as an inspiring role model with her impartial and secular leadership. One of her most important contributions to the freedom struggle was her crucial role in assisting Netaji escape. Due to this, predominantly male associations, like Netaji Bose's All Bengal Young Men's Association, started being renamed in a more inclusive manner, like All Bengal Youth Association. Some groups also started creating sister groups to support these women freedom fighters.

As the freedom struggle reached its final phase, Sabitri Devi's role in the struggle peaked. She became a constant part of the innumerable meetings of the Congress at Anand Bhawan in Allahabad. She was particularly close to the Nehru family, with the late Prime Minister Indira Gandhi referring to her as 'Saili didi'. When freedom finally came on 15 August 1947, Sabitri Devi proudly unfurled the national flag at Kurseong and listened to Nehru's 'Tryst with Destiny' speech on the radio with her fellow countrymen.

After Independence, Sabitri Devi remained involved in numerous causes and supported the efforts of fellow freedom fighters to eradicate social evils such as purdah, untouchability, illiteracy and casteism. She was honoured with the Tamra Patra (Bronze Plaque) award for freedom fighters in 1972, when the Indian Government honoured Indian freedom fighters to mark 25 years of India's Independence. She remained active with a number of groups such as the Sherpa Association, Nagar Congress, Anjuman Islamia, Kurseong Mandal and the Lepcha Association. A true Lepcha all her life, she lived a simple Gandhian life devoid of any luxury until her passing on 18 August 1980, at the age of 78.

# 14

## JAIPAL MUNDA

(1903-1970)

### The Erudite 'Jungli' Lawmaker

It was only apt that the history of India's tribal freedom movement, which started in the second half of the eighteenth century with guerrilla warfare in the jungles of modern-day Jharkhand and Bihar, culminated in the Constituent Assembly during 1946-49, where an Adivasi of rare erudition rendered several epochal speeches that influenced our Constitutional discourse.

On 16 December 1946, Jaipal Singh Munda spoke for the first time in India's Constituent Assembly. He said that he wanted everyone to acknowledge and celebrate some unrecognized freedom warriors, the original people of India who have been known as backward, primitive or criminal tribes and been called by a few other names. He reiterated that he was proud to be a 'Jungli' and it is the name by which his people are known in his part of the country. He pointed out that the tribal people cannot be taught democracy, but the country should learn democratic ways from them. He continued by speaking about the historical exploitation of tribal people, which predated the British rule.[1]

---

[1] '1.9.66 | Mr. Jaipal Singh', Constitution of India, https://bit.ly/37iVSb7. Accessed on 15 April 2022.

Thus, while reminding the nation of the historic injustice that the tribal population had customarily been subjected to over the centuries, Jaipal came across as remarkably pragmatic, conciliatory and positive. As the Constituent Assembly went on to deliberate on other issues of relevance to the Adivasi community in the months to come, Jaipal shone through as an independent thinker and a deft statesman.

For an Adivasi of that generation, Jaipal's nuanced reasoning was indeed rare. A peek into his early years might help in decoding the source of this gravitas.

## Early years

Jaipal was born into a tribal family from the Munda community as Pramod Pahan in Takra Pahantoli, a village in the Khunti subdivision of Ranchi District in Jharkhand (pre-Independence Bengal), on 3 January 1903. Jaipal's parents, like many Adivasi families of the day, had come to embrace Christianity for social peace and in the hope of a better future. As a precocious child, he was noticed by the missionaries in his village at an early age. A group of missionaries affiliated with the Church of England first spotted young Jaipal's leadership qualities, talent and intelligence. He was soon drafted into the missionary-run St Paul's College in Ranchi, where teachers took further note of his intelligence in class and his outstanding talent in hockey. However, how Pramod Pahan was renamed 'Jaipal Munda' will remain in the realm of conjecture.

At 13, Jaipal was sent by local missionaries to Canterbury, followed by Oxford in England to study priesthood. Hockey, though, continued to be a greater attraction for the young Jaipal.

Jaipal's talent in hockey was recognized in England, and he got a chance to not just represent but captain the Indian hockey team at the 1928 Summer Olympics in Amsterdam. At this point, he was under probation as an Indian Civil Service

(ICS) officer in London. But he had to make the difficult choice between playing hockey for India or keeping the prestigious and cosy ICS job. He chose the former.

He then went on to captain the team to its victory march. Unfortunately, the team was not devoid of its class barriers. The selection of Jaipal, an Adivasi, had rubbed many Anglo-Indian players and the team management the wrong way. The differences between both sides resulted in a clash just before the final. After a spat with the team manager, Jaipal pulled out of the final match against Holland. Fortunately, it did not impact the end result as vice-captain Broome Eric Pinniger led the team and clinched the gold medal, a first for India.

Despite this unfortunate episode, then Viceroy of India Lord Irwin congratulated Jaipal for his leadership and the team's win. India's world cup win eventually inspired the India Office to request Jaipal to rejoin the ICS under the condition that they would extend his probation by a year. Jaipal, though, felt that this demand was both insulting and discriminatory, besides being entirely unnecessary.

Unhappy with the prevailing situation, Jaipal rejected a second opportunity to join the ICS and instead joined the multinational oil company, Burmah Shell, where he briefly worked as a senior executive.

However, Jaipal's first and largely unrequited passion remained academia. Thus, he quit his corporate position and took up teaching positions in various colleges across the country. In 1934, he joined the Prince of Wales College at Achimota in Ghana, teaching commerce. Jaipal returned to India in 1937 to become the principal of the Rajkumar College, Raipur, which the *Forward Press* describes as an 'exclusive preserve and grooming ground of young men from Indian princely and feudal families in the company of European students.'[2]

---

[2]Biswas, A. K., 'Jaipal Singh Munda: Hockey champion and the voice of the

Expectedly, Jaipal's subaltern roots and tribal background resulted in discrimination from students and parents alike. After coping with this discrimination for a year, Jaipal joined the administration of the Bikaner Princely State as a revenue commissioner and, subsequently, became the foreign secretary.

## Demand for Jharkhand

In the mid- and late-1930s, Jaipal began his extensive campaign for the rights of the indigenous communities. Around this time, then Governor of Bihar Maurice G. Hallet offered to nominate Jaipal to the Bihar Legislative Assembly, an offer that Jaipal declined. Later, in early 1939, he accepted the leadership of the newly formed Adivasi Sabha (Adivasi Assembly), which he renamed as the Adivasi Mahasabha (Adivasi Grand Assembly). Disillusioned with the inability of the Indian National Congress to advocate for tribal rights more vehemently, Jaipal fought for Adivasi issues through the Adivasi Mahasabha. One of the demands the organization raised was for a separate Adivasi state, which they wanted to be carved out of Bihar and called Jharkhand. This demand of an independent state for tribals raised his stature, and soon, he was being addressed as 'Marang Gomke' or 'great leader' in Mundari, the language of the Munda tribe.

He eventually succeeded in his mission to empower his people when he was elected to the Constituent Assembly from a 'general constituency' in Bihar in 1946. This success led to his epic speech on 9 December 1946, which clearly laid out his agenda for Adivasi empowerment in independent India.

---

voiceless', *Forward Press*, 8 April 2018, https://bit.ly/3uKz4Kr. Accessed on 15 April 2022.

## Adivasi synergy with the nation state

Jaipal's vision for the Adivasis' future in India—in particular, the nature of their relationship with the nation-state—emerges clearly from the speech he delivered in response to the resolution proposed by Nehru regarding India's national flag. He said that he and his people were acknowledging the Indian flag as the country's flag, but reminded those present that it is the tribals who hoisted their flags on various occasions, be it melas, jatras or festivals in Chota Nagpur. Whenever various tribes with their flags entered the arena, each tribe had to come into the jatra by a definite route, and no other tribe could enter the mela by the same route. Each village had its own flag and that flag could not be copied by any other tribe. If anyone dared challenge any flag, that particular tribe would shed its last drop of blood in defending the honour of their flag. Talking of the Indian flag, Jaipal said that the Adivasis of India had accepted and acknowledged the national flag that was presented to them by Pandit Jawaharlal Nehru.[3]

## Opposition to the Fifth Schedule

One of the highlights of Jaipal Munda's innings at the Constituent Assembly was his principled and steadfast opposition, in 1948, to the manner in which the Fifth Schedule was drafted, without giving due weightage to the valid concerns of the stakeholders involved.

The Fifth Schedule, as indicated by its title—Provisions as to the Administration and Control of Scheduled Areas and Scheduled Tribes—applies to many areas formerly classified as 'Excluded' or 'Partially Excluded', including the areas traditionally and predominantly inhabited by tribes that were

---

[3] Kiro, Santosh, *The Life and Times of Jaipal Munda*, Prabhat Prakashan, 2020.

demarcated as special legal and administrative zones by the British administration. Renaming these zones as 'Scheduled Areas', the Fifth Schedule extended the executive power over these zones to the various states within which they were located. Along with the importation of the idea of control over peoples and areas, the rationales and sensibilities that informed the colonial language were also carried over into the Constitution, as indicated by the debate on the Fifth Schedule.

One of Munda's main concerns was that the role and position of the Tribes Advisory Councils (TACs) had been considerably reduced in the proposed Fifth Schedule. He feared that, if accepted, the Fifth Schedule would effectively reduce these TACs to non-entities, making them more of a 'farce'. He said,

> I find that this-new proposed Fifth Schedule has, somehow or other, perhaps without meaning it, emasculated the Tribes Advisory Council. The whole pattern of the original draft was to bring the Tribes Advisory Council into action. It could initiate, originate things, but, somehow or other, the tables have now been turned. The initiative is placed in the hands of the Governor or Ruler of the State. I regret that that is a situation I cannot accept, and, while I say this, Mr. President, I would like to state it is a matter of regret I have to tell the House that, for the last few days secret talks and conferences have been going on among certain people. I have not been consulted. It cannot be said that all parties were consulted. I certainly was not brought to any of those conferences. Suddenly a bomb-shell is thrown by way of the new proposed Fifth Schedule. I do not grumble about the Fifth Schedule. But what I say is there is plenty of scope for improving the Fifth Schedule. I as an Adibasi had and must have the first claim to be consulted in the proposed change.[4]

---

[4]'Constituent Assembly of India, Monday, the 5th September, 1949', https://

Eventually, Jaipal withdrew one of his amendments, while the rest were rejected and the Fifth Schedule was added to the Constitution. Munda's opposition to the Fifth Schedule in the existing form only cemented his stature among the tribal community, besides manifesting his ideological clarity. For someone who was accused by his critics of leading a 'privileged' life compared to the people whose cause he championed, the deliberations over the Fifth Schedule earned his people enormous equity.

## Against prohibition

Jaipal was principally opposed to any prohibition on intoxicating beverages in the Directive Principles of the Constitution. He discussed this in a debate on 24 November 1948, when he spoke of how this provision impinged upon the Adivasi way of life.

> Now, as far as the Adivasis are concerned, no religious function can be performed without the use of rice beer. The word here used—the phrase used is 'intoxicating drinks'. Sir, that is a very vague way of describing the thing, and, also 'injurious to health'. My friend Prof. Shibban Lal has tried to put forward the argument of economic efficiency. He thinks that if prohibition were installed in this country, the economic efficiency of the workers would be enhanced. I dare say it would be. But what I want to tell him is that it is not merely the industrial workers whom he has particularly in mind, that are affected. I would like to point out to him the position of the very poor people, the Adivasis, and, members who come from West Bengal and other places will bear me out in what I say about the Adivasis who are in such large numbers in West Bengal, Southern Bihar, Orissa and other places. In West

---

bit.ly/3qlQfz1. Accessed on 22 March 2022.

Bengal, for instance, it would be impossible for paddy to be transplanted if the Santhal does not get his rice beer.[5]

Jaipal's interventions were crucial in the Constituent Assembly, and led to the idea of including prohibition in the Directive Principles being discarded. The Constituent Assembly inserted multiple constitutional safeguards for the Adivasi communities, acknowledging them as minorities and providing reservation for them in government jobs, among others. This would not have been so seamless without the informed opinion and inputs shared in the Assembly by leaders like Jaipal.

## A prolific legacy

It would be fair to conclude that Jaipal, by virtue of his prolific experiences as a former sportsman, probationary civil servant, corporate executive, followed by being a tribal leader, brought with him a wide gamut of experience. The wealth of his knowledge accorded him an intellectual authority over issues related to tribals, not dissimilar to the one that Ambedkar enjoyed over Dalit issues.

It is a travesty that Jaipal, perhaps because of his free spirit and non-conformist temperament, was not given a position in government commensurate with his knowledge, experience and vision. His legacy has sadly been ignored by most tribal leaders who held sway over the Adivasi discourse post Independence.

He always insisted on the need to be sensitive to tribal cultures. The significant role he played in highlighting the concerns of Adivasis and their demands for justice across India appears to have been largely ignored by legal researchers. Despite his presence in the Assembly, his speeches and silences

---

[5] Arora, Sakshi, 'This Tribal Leader Who Opposed Prohibition Also Led India to First Olympic Hockey Gold', *The Print*, 14 August 2018, https://bit.ly/3ufwkmE. Accessed on 22 March 2022.

and his claims and disagreements that offer insights into the possibilities and limits of justice for Adivasis as the original inhabitants of this nation, Jaipal remains absent from the history of the Indian constitution.

### Bidding adieu

On 19 March 1970, Jaipal returned to Delhi after finishing some work in Calcutta. The next morning, a few friends visited him. Little did they know that it would turn out to be a farewell visit. When the domestic staff went to inform Jaipal of the visitors, he realized that his employer had been in the bath for an unusually long time. Upon breaking in, he found Jaipal lying dead on the floor after having suffered a cerebral haemorrhage. His mortal remains were flown to Takra Pahantoli, where he was buried.

Jaipal Munda's articulation on issues of importance to the Adivasi community has been the most nuanced, pragmatic and progressive in the annals of our Parliamentary democracy.

Jaipal's oratory in 1948–49 in the Constituent Assembly, when seen in the context of the jungle warfare first witnessed in the revolution of Tilka Manjhi in 1784, marked the coming of age of India's subaltern freedom movement. In a way, it set the trajectory for the Adivasi population to be a cohesive part of the country's mainstream.

## 15

## RANI GAIDINLIU

(1915-1993)

### Joan of Arc in the Land of Gems

On 29 August 1931, under false charges of murder, Haipou Jadonang was arrested by the British and hanged on the banks of the Nambul River behind the Imphal jail in Manipur. Originally an ascetic belonging to the Zeliangrong/Zeme family of tribes, he founded Heraka, a socio-religious reform movement with the dual intention of making their indigenous religion as relevant as Christianity, which was being propagated by the missionaries, and ousting the British from the region. This made Jadonang a *maiba*, a leading priest of the clan, and many of his followers turned up to pay their last respects before he was sent to the gallows. Among them was his 16-year-old cousin Gaidinliu.

Unlike the public that had assembled, Gaidinliu watched from a distance, camouflaged to avoid being detected by the authorities. She had narrowly escaped getting caught by them when they had arrested Jadonang in February that year, when the two of them, along with their followers, were on a pilgrimage to the revered Bhuban caves located in the hills of North Cachar in Assam.

With Jadonang gone, the responsibility of keeping the Heraka movement alive now rested on Gaidinliu, not just because of her filial connection with him but also because she had been his trusted lieutenant. Jadonang had groomed her for this. Both of them were mystics of sorts. While Jadonang professed to have been bestowed with divine powers by Tingkao Ragwang, the Kabui supreme being, Gaidinliu spoke of being personally guided by a goddess that was sacred to the Bhuban Hills, the same place where Jadonang had been allegedly baptised by Tingkao Ragwang. She was given cups of healing water from the Bhuban cave, using which she healed many people. In fact, it is said that during Jadonang's baptism, he was given the same healing water to drink. Both chose to write their teachings in a lost, sacred script, one that they received from Tingkao Ragwang directly; both were humiliated by the British for doing so.[1]

## A sacred birth and early childhood

Gaidinliu was born to Lothonang Pamei and Kachotlenliu, a Rongmei/Kabui family that lived in Nungkoa village (also called Lungkao), located in the Tousem subdivision of Tamenglong district in present-day Manipur, on 26 January 1915. As she was born with the umbilical cord twisting itself around her neck, the *maibas* (priests) and *maibis* (priestesses) present on occasion prophesized that the child would grow up to be extraordinary—she did.

She grew up as per the tradition for the girls of her clan learning weaving, farming and music, which would eventually prepare her for marriage. However, by the age of 13, she had started having preternatural experiences, mostly as visions and dreams. A recurring theme in these was Gaidinliu entering into the discipleship of a mystic. It is believed that through these

---

[1]Longkumer, Arkotong, "'Lines that speak": The Gaidinliu notebooks as language, prophecy, and textuality', *Journal of Ethnographic Theory*, Vol. 6, No. 2, 2016, pp. 123-147, DOI:10.14318/hau6.2.011.

visions and dreams, she realized that her cousin, Jadonang, was the mystic, and she was destined to become his disciple. This led to her meeting him in 1926 at Kambiron, Assam.

Upon meeting Jadonang, she was immediately accepted as his disciple. Under his tutelage, Gaidinliu came to learn of the larger significance of the Heraka movement, which was uniting the three tribes—Zeme, Liangmai and Rongmei/Kabui— that lived across Assam, Nagaland and Manipur and whose common ancestry could be traced to the Munhu-Nguiba tribe from Makuilongdi village, in the Senapati district of Manipur.[2] Post 1947, to show their connectedness, they started using the prefix Zeliangrong, a combination of the three prefixes of these tribes, Ze-liang-rong. The presence of the opportunist Christian missionaries and the rise of the culturally ignorant British administration made it difficult to achieve this. Thus, establishing a 'Naga Raj' was core to the movement.

## Heraka and Naga Raj

By the time Gaidinliu joined Jadonang, he had already raised an armed force of around 500 trained youths, called Riphen. The Riphen worked at two levels. First, they protested against land revenue, house taxes and the illegal practice of long-abolished *Pothang Bekahri/Pothang Senkhai*[3]—a form of forced labour— which required an entire village to offer its services when the

---

[2]Niumai, Ajailiu, 'Rani Gaidinliu: The Iconic Woman of Northeast India', *Indian Journal of Gender Studies*, Vol. 25, No. 3, 2018, pp. 351–367.

[3]'Pothang literally means pot (baggage) and thang (to carry). Under Manipuri law, every village had to cater for the visiting king, members of his family, and state officials when they toured the village or the region. This was abolished in 1913, with the help of the British, but the practice continued illegally in some regions' (Qtd. in Longkumer, Arkotong, 'Religious and Economic Reform: The Gaidinliu Movement and the Heraka in the North Cachar Hills', *Journal of South Asian Studies*, Vol. 30, No. 3, 499–515, https://bit.ly/3It4V5E. Accessed on 21 March 2022).

king or members of the royal family or state officials visited them. Second, they coaxed clansmen who had abandoned their original faith to become Presbyterian, Baptist or Catholic, to return to it.

However, what caught the eye of the administration was the Heraka agenda of the geographical unification of the dispersed tribes. The message of the movement spread like wildfire and started to become a cause of serious concern to the British, with the political agent[4] of Manipur, John Comyn Higgins, labelling it an insurgency.[5] But Higgins' opinion on the Heraka and the Zeliangrongs was worse than this. He regarded the tribes as beings with no intelligence and, hence, without any right to fight. It was, thus, his suggestion that military force be used to quell the movement that chose to counter colonial expansionism through cultural resources of language and mysticism. Higgins began by destroying the temples that had been built by Jadonang for worship. Although, this didn't deter Jadonang, with his death, it appeared as if the British had won.

### Gaidinliu takes over

Unfortunately, for the British, they had grossly underestimated the influence of Gaidinliu and the power of Heraka that she was about to exude. Her petite, 5-feet-tall external appearance was quite unlike her indomitable inner strength and tremendous courage. It is from this space that she found the determination to encourage her people to oppose the oppressive British administration that had made it a routine to use forced labour, collect revenue taxes from each house in every village, feast at the expense of the poor villagers, construct inter-village roads

---

[4]Someone who runs the administration of the local kingdom on behalf of the British, under the pretext of assisting the local king.

[5]Niumai, Ajailiu, 'Rani Gaidinliu: The Iconic Woman of Northeast India', *Indian Journal of Gender Studies*, Vol. 25, No. 3, 2018, pp. 351-367.

and bungalows made of bamboo and thatch roofs to stay for a single night in the village at no cost, and have themselves carried in bamboo palanquins when the roads were rough to walk on. Coming from a community whose law and culture prohibited women from participating in any decision-making processes, inheriting property or fighting with weapons against enemies, Gaidinliu set about empowering girls and young women with the *dao*—the traditional spear used by her community to fight. To her followers, she was an incarnation of their goddess Cherachamdinliu who possessed supernatural powers that could cause miraculous healing. Although she had no formal education, as a child, she had convinced her mother to get school notebooks from Kohima and filled about a dozen of them with what she claimed was 'dictation from her spirit guides'.[6] These actions only bolstered the belief of Gaidinliu being a superwoman.

The many songs that she composed chronicled how Heraka would usher in the lost 'golden age' of the Zeliangrongs.[7] These songs used themes and stories of mythic heroes and folklores of the tribes. In these songs and stories, the heroes always celebrated the events that were bringing about the change that ultimately led to joy and abundance. Heraka allowed its followers to move out of their villages, get educated and find jobs. It encouraged people to enhance their social status. Since Heraka originated in Vaishnavism, it encouraged acting in a manner befitting a Hindu society. All these activities also aimed to suppress the superiority of those who had converted to Christianity.

---

[6]Longkumer, Arkotong, '"Lines that speak": The Gaidinliu notebooks as language, prophecy, and textuality', *Journal of Ethnographic Theory*, Vol. 6, No. 2, 2016, pp. 123-147, DOI:10.14318/hau6.2.011.

[7]Niumai, Ajailiu, 'Rani Gaidinliu: The Iconic Woman of Northeast India', *Indian Journal of Gender Studies*, Vol. 25, No. 3, 2018, pp. 351-367.

## Destabilizing the government with resistance

Within a few weeks of Jadanong's death in 1931, the movement regained its earlier momentum. Alarmed, the British took to defaming Gaidinliu publicly and questioned her credibility. Deputy Commissioner J.P. Mills of the Naga Hills District, claimed that Gaidinliu was only after name and fame and, to do so, she was styling herself as a sorceress and selling 'bottled water' from the stream that flowed near the Bhuban caves. Higgins shared details about Gaidinliu with John Henry Hutton, a political officer posted in Assam, who later turned into a full-time anthropologist. Hutton accused her of gathering a large number of followers so that they could spy on the Kuki tribe, against whom the Zeliangrongs had grievances regarding land ownership, under the pretext of miraculous healing. According to him, ever since the Kukis had occupied the land of the Zeliangrongs, after the latter had abandoned it as part of their practice of shifting cultivation, the tribes had been at war. He conveniently chose to overlook the fact that it was his own administration that had allotted the land to the Kukis and encouraged them to stay put by tempting them with free training on modern agricultural practices.

However, despite all the slandering, it became increasingly evident to the British government that the movement was growing stronger by the day and it could definitely be detrimental to them in the long run.

## The relentless chase and arrest

In February 1932, Gaidinliu and her followers attacked the Assam Rifles outpost at Hungrum, in the hills of North Cachar, killing six soldiers and injuring numerous others. In retaliation, a massive manhunt was launched to capture the 17-year-old Gaidinliu who had, by that time, focused her attention on the

Tamenglong district of Manipur, south Nagaland and the North Cachar Hills of Assam. To expedite her arrest, Mills announced a cash award of 500 rupees while the Manipur Durbar announced reward of 200 rupees for anyone who would supply information that would lead to her arrest. Additionally, a Christian convert from the Pulomi village, Dr Haralu, also announced an award of 100 rupees.[8] However, these incentives failed to lure anyone. So, Mills offered a 10-year tax break to anybody or any village that would become willing informants. Still, there were no leads. On the contrary, on March 1932, Gaidinliu struck again, nearly destroying the Assam Rifles' outpost that had been set up to patrol the area as part of the search operations to hunt down Gaidinliu. The tedious chase continued.

Ultimately, in October 1932, Gaidinliu moved to the Pulomi village situated in the Peren district of Nagaland. Deputy Commissioner Mills was already aware of the threat of Gaidinliu's presence to his administration. Hence, both security and search activities were doubled. Gaidinliu's agenda here was to build a fortress that could hold 4,000 of her warriors. While this fortress was being constructed, word about it reached Dr Haralu, who lost no time informing Hari Blah, the additional Assistant Commissioner at Kohima, who, in turn, informed Mills. A plan was drawn. On 17 October 1932, Captain MacDonald, along with a 100-member contingent of the Assam Rifles, launched a surprise attack and arrested Gaidinliu. Mills immediately started a trial against her and she was jailed in Kohima for two months. Subsequently, she was deported to Imphal, where Higgins charged her with murder and starting a revolt against the British Crown. On 7 March 1933, aged 18 years, she was sentenced to life imprisonment.

As she was being taken away, Higgins not only ordered

---

[8]Idlet, John Thomas, *Evangelising the Nation: Religion and the Formation of Naga Political Identity*, Routledge, 2015.

the confiscation of her personal items like clothing, shawls and jewellery, but also the notebooks that had her writing. He feared that in her absence, the Heraka followers would keep the movement alive by religiously following what she had penned in the books. However, Higgins did not destroy them. Being a curiosity collector, he kept them with him and, today, these books, along with the original basket in which they were kept, can be viewed in the Pitt Rivers Museum, England.

With Gaidinliu out of action, the government set about eradicating all traces of the Heraka movement and its followers. Villages were burnt down and properties destroyed, and the followers were either tortured or killed. The few who escaped were from the Leng and Bopungwemi villages. These few followers investigated how their leader had been betrayed and found that it was the doing of a Kuki chowkidar (watchman) of the Lakema Inspection Bungalow in the Naga Hills. He had acted as an informer for the British. The Heraka followers killed him.

Immediately after her prison sentence was announced, Gaidinliu was shifted to the Guwahati jail. During this time, a mercy petition was filed to the Governor of Assam. This was rejected and, after about a year, she was shifted to the Tura jail in present-day Meghalaya. It was here that Jawaharlal Nehru met her during his Assam tour in 1937. Impressed with her bravery and determination in her efforts to oust the British, he honoured her with the title 'Rani' and attempted to secure her release through the first female MP in British history, Lady Nancy Astor. This request, too, was shot down and Gaidinliu continued to languish in jail until Independence.

## Against Naga sovereignty

After India gained Independence, Nehru, the first prime minister of the nation, ordered the Assam government to release Gaindinliu. On 14 October 1947, at the age of 32, she emerged from Tura district jail, a free warrior, and went to live with her younger brother at Vimrap village in the Makunkchung district of Nagaland. The government had placed numerous restrictions on her movement that prevented her from visiting her native village, but that did not stop her from taking forward the cause of the Zeliangrongs. She realized that now was the time to press forward with the remaining goal of the Heraka—a state for the Zeliangrongs, under the banner of the Zeliangrong People Convention (ZPC)—since it had been relegated to only being a religion with the intention of outdoing Christianity. The ZPC only sought statehood while remaining a part of India. Once the restrictions on her movement were lifted in 1952, not only was she able to visit her native village in Imphal but was also able to initiate and maintain contact with the central government. She met the first president, Dr Rajendra Prasad, and Prime Minister Nehru. In her meetings, she put forward her demands for socio-economic welfare programmes for the Zeliangrongs.

This was in stark contrast to the ideology of those Nagas who, upon conversion to Christianity and/or having fought in the First World War, had come to believe that they were a unique set of people that neither identified with the British nor the Indians and were entitled to a country of their own. This demand for Naga sovereignty that had started in 1918 under the Naga Club, later the Naga Peoples' Convention (NPC), ignored the Zeliangrongs, who refused to believe in the superiority of the Western culture and Christian religion. Gaindinliu was not at all in favour of such a sovereign nation. The rift clearly began to show after Independence. In the mid-1950s, the friction between the two factions intensified to the point that Gaidinliu began to be regarded as an obstacle towards attaining the NPC's goal, and she started receiving death threats again.

In a repetition of previous incidents, she went into hiding and raised an army while remaining underground. Not only did she raise an army of 1,000 strong men, the Kampai, but she was also able to source modern weaponry that had been retired from the Second World War. In 1962, violence broke out between the ZPC and the NPC. Due to the conflict, the nearly 45-year-old Gaidinliu went into hiding in the rock cave at Mount Kisha near Magulong village in Tamenglong district, which could shelter up to 200 people.[9] The hideout provided for the need of the hour and was aptly named—Mount Kisha, which means 'Mount of the God of Wars'.[10] She stayed there for three years. Finally, in January 1966, upon the mediation of the Nagaland and Manipur governments through Subodh Chandra Dev, the deputy commissioner of Kohima, Gaidinliu agreed to end the warfare and start negotiations.

After three long days of discussion, she secured a meeting with the then Prime Minister Indira Gandhi. In this meeting, she and her people intended to submit a memorandum demanding a separate 'Zeliangrong Administrative Unit' under the Union of India. She was given assurance for this meeting in writing. Accordingly, on 22 February 1966, she met with Indira Gandhi. From then on, Gaidinliu tirelessly pursued every prime minister who came to power in her lifetime. Displaying great foresight, she also forged good relationships with the Bharatiya Janata Party (BJP) and its allies—the Vishwa Hindu Parishad (VHP) and Rashtriya Swayamsevak Sangh (RSS).

## In pursuit of true nationalism

Gaidinliu's relentless fight against foreign culture and religion established her as a true nationalist and she received the highest possible respect for this—she was provided with a bungalow, security, VIP status and a freedom fighter's pension.

---

[9]Singh, Hitler, 'In the Den of Rani Gaidinliu the Legendary Freedom Fighter—Mount Kisha at Magulong Village', E-Pao, https://bit.ly/3xrwkTH. Accessed on 14 April 2022.

[10]Currently, it is referred to as Gaidinliu Den.

She continued to pursue the cause of a separate homeland for her people until her passing on 17 February 1993. The inconclusiveness of the issue and the NPC's policy of isolating her exist even today. This notably came to fore during her birth centenary in 2015, when the BJP-led government put forward the proposal of constructing a library-cum-memorial museum to mark the occasion in Kohima, Nagaland. The mainstream Naga leaders criticized the move, calling her a witch and cannibal.

Nevertheless, her people remember her not merely as an aggressive freedom fighter but also as a deeply spiritual, kind-hearted woman who treasured life, was protective of her clansmen and enjoyed the simple pleasures of life.

In 1996, acknowledging her contributions, the government of India released a one rupee postage stamp in her honour. Although she has since been decorated with many prestigious awards, one that stands out the most is the naming of a naval patrol vessel launched by the Indian Coast Guard in 2016 after her. It has been a fitting tribute to one of the most courageous women of the country.

# 16

## DASHRIBEN CHAUDHURY

(1918–2013)

### The Courage of a Disobedient Girl

Viceroy Lord Irwin's failure to provide dominion status to India by 31 December 1929 pushed Mahatma Gandhi to launch a nationwide civil disobedience movement. He started it by breaking the tax on salt. On the morning of 12 March 1930, he set out for Dandi from his Sabarmati Ashram, along with a group of 79 satyagrahis, both men and women. As the group walked forward, the number of satyagrahis grew steadily, so that by the time they approached Surat, the Mahatma was leading a 3-kilometre-long line of satyagrahis. In Surat, as in several places before this, they were joined by another group of satyagrahis. One of them was Rusmibhai Chaudhury, a teacher who had come with nine others from Vedchhi, a village situated in the present-day Tapi district, 60 kilometres east of Surat, Gujarat.

Rusmibhai was a Kaliparaj, an Adivasi from a relatively higher social rank that had the privilege of receiving education, by virtue of which he was well-informed on current affairs. He, along with his brothers, had taken after his father Jeevanbhai Chaudhury, an educated man himself, and had become a teacher. Owing to this privileged background, the women of the household enjoyed a far better status than others. This also meant that they had access to education. Rusmibhai's daughter Dashri was one of them.

## A child satyagrahi

At the time of the Dandi Salt March, Dashri had been studying in a school in Pune headed by Kasturba Gandhi, where one of her uncles was a teacher. She learnt about satyagraha and the call for civil disobedience when a letter from Mahatma Gandhi addressed to Kasturba arrived at the school in early March 1930.[1] In it, he asked the girls of the school to contribute to the salt satyagraha by spreading its message to the nearby villages. Dashri was barely 12 at the time but not new to the fight against the British.

Earlier, in 1928, during the Bardoli Satyagraha, Dashri had gone from village to village narrating stories of the atrocities committed by the British and singing patriotic songs to spread the message of satyagraha. Owing to her formal education, she was able to speak to the villagers in both the Adivasi dialect and Gujarati whenever required. Also, along with her friends, Dashri had picketed liquor shops and destroyed toddy palm trees and fruits to protest against the government's policy of prohibiting the tribals from producing and selling toddy while actively encouraging its consumption. This new excise policy, known as the 'Madras System', aimed to keep the tribals addicted to drinking just for the sake of generating revenue. If they objected, then the upper caste people and British administrative officers would force liquor down their throats.

---

[1] Sharma, Jyotirmaya, 'This Girl Is Very Dangerous', Debating India, 10 April 2005, https://bit.ly/3Ntp5Ag. Accessed on 15 April 2022.

## An 'awakening' among the Kaliparajs

The Kaliparajs had always been forest dwellers and had largely lived by tilling their own land and living off forest produce. But with the arrival of the Bania and Parsi moneylenders during the rule of Sayajirao Gaekwad III, the ruler of Baroda, they started to lose their land. Furthermore, they were cheated of their remaining land with the onset of the money-based economy introduced by the British administration, which the tribals were not adept at, and through the Indian Forest Act (1878) and the Land Acquisition Act (1894). The tribals then found themselves working as domestic help or agricultural labourers, receiving little or no wages. What they still managed to retain was their toddy drinking habit, an addiction so strong that it had reduced them to asking for credit to buy drinks.

When the First World War commenced, it caused cotton prices to shoot up. That's when this illiterate section among the Kaliparaj made a lot of money. However, they used it unwisely, spending it on purchasing houses, land and extravagant weddings. When the war ended, their earnings went down but their expenses did not. To meet their expenditure and daily needs, especially that of toddy drinking, they sold off their belongings. Already illiterate and now moneyless and landless, the tribals were reduced to living in deplorable conditions. Gradually, superstition took over and their decimation was complete.

The higher castes among the Adivasis, such as the Dhodias, Gamits and Chaudharys—the tribe to which Dashri belonged—had fared better. They took advantage of the dedicated boarding schools opened by Sayajirao for the Kaliparaj society and sent their children to get educated. Here, along with education and boarding facilities, the young boys and girls learnt the basics of hygiene as well as received clothing and essential items like soap and hair oil. These families firmly believed in using education to progress their lives, families and society. In 1903, under the leadership of Dashri's grandfather, the Kaliparaj Parishad or the Black People's/Forest People's Conference was organized in Vedchhi, to which Mahatma Gandhi was invited. However, it was Kasturba who came to attend it.

Mahatma Gandhi's visit finally materialized in 1924, two years after the Swaraj Ashram had been established in Bardoli. He revisited in 1926. Dashri was eight years old during the Mahatma's second visit. Yet, she registered the full import of what he was talking about. After Gandhi finished his speech, little Dashri rushed up the dais to him and handed over every piece of jewellery that she was wearing. It was her contribution to the Tilak Swaraj Fund, which Gandhi had established as a homage to Bal Gangadhar Tilak on his first death anniversary. He had aimed to raise one crore rupees, which was to be used for various activities supporting India's freedom struggle.

Made only of silver, brass and nickel, the jewellery did not amount to much monetarily. Yet, the act of Dashri willingly giving up these precious items had a powerful impact. It led to all the women who had come to attend the meeting to deposit their jewellery as well. With this began a long-term association of the Vedchhi women with Kasturba—especially between Kasturba and Dashri.

## Becoming 'disobedient'

The act of illegally producing salt as part of the Dandi March came at a great cost to the satyagrahis. The police mercilessly beat them and had them jailed. Dashri's father, along with her uncles, was arrested and imprisoned at the Yerawada jail in Pune. In 1933, after her father was released, Dashri went with six other women to Surat to picket in front of a shop that sold clothes made in Manchester. She had a board around her neck that read, 'Civil Disobedience'.

Soon, a police officer tied her up in cords and, pointing a rifle at her chest, asked her to swear that she would never again take Gandhi's name and give up spinning, weaving and wearing khadi. Dashri promptly disagreed to all these demands, whereupon she was arrested and produced before a magistrate for trial. Her replies to the questions asked by the magistrate were remarkable for her age and background.

'What is your name?'
'Dashriben Rusmibhai', she replied.
'Where do you live?'
'India.'
'Where do you work?'
'India.'
'What will you do now?'
'Get Swaraj.'

The magistrate then said, 'This girl is very dangerous. She hasn't given even a single straight reply!' He continued, 'What is your age?'

She said, 'How do I know? We are Adivasis. We don't know how to read or write.'

'Do you promise not to spin and wear khadi and promise not to utter Gandhi's name?' The magistrate asked.

'I will do all this. We have come here to take Swaraj. Whether we live or die, until the time we do not get Swaraj, we will do exactly this,' she replied defiantly.[2]

Her defiance was rewarded with a sentence of one-year rigorous imprisonment, which she served first at the Sabarmati jail and later at Yerawada jail.

---

[2]Barla, Alma Grace, *Indigenous Heroines: A Saga of Tribal Women of India*, IWGIA, 2015, p. 53.

## Meeting Kasturba in jail

At the Yerawada jail, children imprisoned for their participation in the disobedience movement were assigned the task of preparing tamarind pulp, just like the women. The children were also allotted daily individual quotas that each had to meet. Dashri had to prepare 20 kilograms of tamarind pulp. At barely 14 years old, she was unfamiliar with this activity and failed to meet her daily target once. As a punishment, the jail superintendent did not allow dinner to be served to her. Word of this incident spread fast throughout the jail and reached Kasturba. It was Kasturba's daily routine to eat only after everyone else had eaten. So, when she heard about Dashri, she declared that unless the child was given food, she would not touch hers. Eventually, this turned into a fast until the superintendent agreed to withdraw Dashri's punishment. The worm-infested watery soup and grit-mixed rice and vegetables were by no means a decent meal, but for a hungry 14-year-old in jail, it was needed for sustenance.

Dashri always recalled this incident with great reverence for Kasturba. In many ways, Dashri came to resemble her. Just like Kasturba, Dashri too stood barely five feet tall and still managed to appear far taller by standing quite upright and tall. The many years spent with Kasturba also led Dashri to speak and gesture in similar ways. It was through Kasturba that the women of Vedchhi embraced Gandhi's teaching about truth and non-violence.

## Teaching Kasturba

Shortly after the fasting episode, Kasturba met Dashri during their designated free hour in the evening, when all prison inmates were allowed to walk in the courtyard. Kasturba used this opportunity to teach women to pray and stay motivated.

During this meeting, Kasturba expressed her desire to learn to read and write. Although she was never a shy leader, Kasturba sensed her illiteracy as a handicap during press meets. More importantly, in that moment, she was finding it increasingly difficult to communicate with her husband, who was also lodged in the same jail. They could only communicate by writing letters, and Kasturba always had to ask for help.

Initially, Dashri felt a little awkward at this request, as she felt that having studied only till fifth grade, she wasn't educated enough to be teaching others. However, Kasturba assured Dashri that her level of education was all she needed. So, arranging for a primer, the two set to work despite the fact that Kasturba was kept in the A-class prison while Dashri was in the C-class. They progressed fast and, soon, Dashri was guiding Kasturba on how to write letters. The real test came when, one day, Kasturba had to write to Mahatma Gandhi. Kasturba didn't feel confident about doing this on her own. 'Ba, you write. If you make mistakes, I'll help you correct them,' Dashri assured her.[3] Encouraged, Kasturba drafted her first letter ever. Dashri made corrections and then Kasturba copied the final version in her own handwriting.

Gandhi received this letter with great astonishment. He wrote back, thoroughly impressed at Kasturba's efforts, reminiscing his failed attempts to teach her when they had been living in South Africa. 'When I used to teach you, I used to get irritated and you used to break into tears. Now, who has managed to teach you how to write? How did you manage to learn?' Kasturba wrote back telling him about Dashri. To this, he replied, 'Really, this girl has taught you? Well done, give this girl my grateful thanks.'[4]

---

[3]Sharma, Jyotirmaya, 'This Girl Is Very Dangerous', Debating India, 10 April 2005, https://bit.ly/3Ntp5Ag. Accessed on 28 March 2022.
[4]Ibid.

## Independence and after

After her jail term ended, Dashri returned to Sabarmati Ashram and completed her studies. Simultaneously, she participated in and contributed to the freedom struggle. When the Quit India movement was announced in Bardoli in August 1942, Dashri led 5,000 people to the police station in Bardoli, where she intended to hoist the tricolour.[5] However, the group was intercepted before they could reach the police station. Dashri was arrested and, once again, sent to Yerawada jail. Upon her release in early 1944, she married Kanjibhai Chaudhary, a fellow freedom fighter. On 22 February 1944, Kasturba died at the Aga Khan Palace in Pune. This impacted Dashri quite strongly and, thereafter, she dedicated her life to teaching Adivasi children and youth along with her husband.

Dashri retired as a teacher in 1976. After that, she became the president of the Gujarat Khadi Gram Udyog, an organization tasked with promoting handwoven khadi or cotton garments and other items. She remained an active member of this organization until the death of her husband in 1998. Since then, until her own passing on 2 September 2013 in Vedchhi, she worked as an active member of the Adivasi Ekta Parishad, an Adivasi council that worked towards promoting tribal culture.

---

[5]Barla, Alma Grace, *Indigenous Heroines: A Saga of Tribal Women of India*, IWGIA, 2015, p. 53.

# 17

## PUTALIMAYA DEVI

(1920–1984)

### Challenging Patriarchy and the British

An air of tension enveloped the Gorkha Jan Pustakalaya in Kurseong, even though the occasion was a happy one. It was 1944, and a young couple was getting married. Both had just been released from prison for participating in the Quit India movement. The bride, Putalimaya Devi Tamang, was the daughter of a Gorkha peon working at a subdivisional office. The groom, Saryu Prasad Poddar, was a zamindar turned Congress activist from Bihar. Even the Kurseong winter could not allay the heat that was brewing from the anger towards this inter-caste marriage. Such was the displeasure that some goons from the area—Hanseh and Bhombey—showed up at the wedding venue wielding kukris, the traditional Nepali dagger, and threatened the couple. Luckily for them, the presence of Chandra Devi Pradhan, a fellow freedom fighter, along with her cousin and aunt, each of whom was armed with a kukri as well, warded off the thugs.[1] The ceremony was concluded in peace,

---

[1] Pakhrin, Kalyani, 'Challenging the Hegemons: The Unheard Story of a Brave Woman, Putalimaya Devi Poddar', *IOSR Journal of Humanities and Social Science (IOSR-JHSS)*, Vol. 10, No. 2, 2013, pp. 53–60.

although the couple was yet to conquer various struggles, chief among them—India's freedom from the British.

## The initial soul stirring

Putalimaya was born on 14 January 1920 to Mann Bahadur Tamang and his wife. She was the eldest of four daughters. Mann Bahadur worked as a watchman with the Kurseong municipality. Owing to his Nepali origin, he was regarded as a loyal employee serving British officials.[2] A diligent employee at work, he was the quintessential Nepali head of the family at home, ensuring that the women kept busy with domestic chores, not bothering themselves with the mess of the world outside. However, his increasing interactions with the newly evolving society in Darjeeling and Kalimpong made him a bit more modern in his approach towards women's equality. As a result, he was supportive of providing a good education to his daughters. Putalimaya, thus, had the luxury of studying at the Scott Mission School in Kurseong. At home, though, she had to devote time to assisting her mother with household chores and when her mother fell sick, household chores became her full-time responsibility. She would attend her classes only after she had finished her household chores and tended to her younger sisters and father.

She was aware that, given her domestic responsibilities, she should not dabble much with worldly affairs. However, the prevailing situation was such that it was impossible to keep away from the political activities aimed at attaining Independence. Already, the likes of Sabitri Devi (née Helen Lepcha), Harish Chettri and Dal Bahadur Giri had motivated the people of Kurseong, Kalimpong and Darjeeling to join the freedom struggle.

---

[2] Ibid.

At the age of 14, in 1934, Putalimaya had the opportunity to attend a mass meeting. The speaker of this meeting was a young Congress leader from Bihar, Saryu Prasad Poddar. Dressed in khadi, he cut an impressive figure as he awakened the latent patriots in the audience with his Gandhian philosophy. At the end of this meeting, everyone at the meeting expressed their support and desire to participate in the Independence movement. Putalimaya was among them. In fact, she wanted to join the Congress. However, given that the British were strictly surveilling the inhabitants of the region, it was dangerous for the hill folks to openly embrace and flaunt their association with either the Congress or anything even remotely related to Indian independence. To top it all off, Putalimaya was still a student in her teens.

As a result, Saryu Prasad was unwilling to accept her. Instead, he suggested that she continue her studies until it was the right time for her to join the movement.

Putalimaya was disappointed. However, she did not let it come in the way of expressing her patriotic self. She decided to offer support through social service and participated in various meetings while attending school. This angered her family, as they were totally against her interest in the freedom struggle. Her father admonished her and asked her to stay away from these activities. But Putalimaya's heart was set. Soon, she found a workable solution to her problem. After her father went to work, she would begin her patriotic activities. She started by organizing secret meetings and becoming a messenger for confidential information. Next, she started a night school, the Harijan Samaj, for socially and economically backward women and children, where she taught them to read and write and made them aware of the ill effects of alcoholism.

## The plunge

In 1936, the Kurseong branch of the Congress committee was launched. This time, Putalimaya was much more vocal about her intentions with her family. Once more, they disapproved of her choice. Adding to her woes was the warning that she received from the administration as well. In fact, to permanently dissuade her from the path, they offered her a lucrative job as a nurse at the district hospital. Putalimaya rejected both the warning and the job offer to boldly step into a territory unknown to her conservative folks.

Now that she was formally a part of the Congress, she started receiving detailed training on how to conduct welfare activities. Learning to spin the charkha and weave khadi was at the core of this training. When she set up the Nari Kalyan Samiti in 1939, this training greatly helped her empower women to become economically independent. This was a significant initiative because, at that time, it was left to the women of the family to keep the household running while the men went out for political errands.

Both the Harijan Samaj and Nari Kalyan Samiti quickly gained popularity among the common people. They also became important mediums through which the Gandhian principles for achieving freedom could be spread far and wide. Due to these untiring initiatives of Putalimaya, women in the region soon started promoting the nationalist movement and showing their allegiance to Mahatma Gandhi. Some of them even started keeping a photograph of Mahatma Gandhi in their shrine at home, regarding him as a messiah.

As the popularity of Putalimaya's work increased, so did the warnings from the British officials and her family to keep away. However, Putalimaya remained unfazed and focused on her work.

## Quit India

The Quit India movement was launched on 8 August 1942. On 9 August, several Congress leaders in Kurseong were arrested as a precautionary measure. However, it neither derailed nor dampened the spirit of the protestors. As per the plan for the region, on 12 August, Saryu Prasad took out a rally of 1,000 people with the aim of disrupting every bit of government machinery that showed up along their route. The rally involved intense sloganeering, raids on shops and picketing and gheraoing of police stations. In an attempt to curb the protest, the police arrested Saryu Prasad. In retaliation, Putalimaya organized a fresh protest the very next day to keep the momentum of the movement going. It resulted in her getting arrested as well. All the arrested leaders were taken to Darjeeling jail, where they were asked to sign a letter stating that they would not be participating in such activities again. When they refused to comply, they were treated as ordinary criminals and lodged in jail indefinitely.

Putalimaya protested at not being treated like a political prisoner. Unhappy about this, she went on a hunger strike. During this time, her health started failing. As her health continued to deteriorate, she was released in January 1944. Shortly after, Saryu Prasad was also released.

Upon release, Putalimaya was disowned by her family, as they felt deeply hurt by her refusal to abide by their requests. They served her with an ultimatum—she was to choose her family or the movement. The brave young woman chose patriotism over family. However, in her orthodox society, it was not going to be easy for a single woman to live by herself. Sensing this situation, the senior leaders of the Congress suggested that she get married to Saryu Prasad.

The Nepali community, in which the caste system was observed strictly, disapproved of a Nepali woman marrying a Marwari. According to the community, while marriage was an important aspect of an individual's social life, it had to be within the same caste. Else, one had to face alienation from both the family as well as society. Putalimaya's admirable patriotic contributions did nothing to soften this stance. On the day of the wedding, she was deprived of her family's presence as well as blessings. But for Chandra Devi Pradhan and her aunt's support and affection, this new part of Putalimaya's life would not have been initiated. In fact, Chandra Devi's aunt had come to regard Saryu Prasad as her son and during troubled times, she helped them financially as well. There were days in the life of the newly married couple when they had to go without food. However, the couple never let these struggles dishearten them and neither did they stop participating in the last stage of the freedom struggle.

### Independent India

Post 1947, Putalimaya continued her social service along with serving as an active Congress member. She became the president of the Mahukuma Congress Committee of Kurseong and the vice-president of the Darjeeling District Committee. Later on, she also took up the cause of the women who worked in tea estates. In 1975, her contribution towards the freedom struggle was recognized by the Indian Government by awarding her the Tamra Patra and the Swatantrata Sainik Samman Pension Scheme (freedom fighter's pension).[3] Putalimaya was fondly addressed as 'Mata ji' for her work with the poor and underprivileged. She breathed her last on 1 December 1984 at a hospital in Siliguri.

---

[3]Sharma, Suryamani (ed.), *Hamra Swantantrata Senani*, Sumeru Publication, Siliguri, 1990, p. 76.

# ACKNOWLEDGEMENTS

The authors are grateful to PM Narendra Modi for drawing the nation's attention towards our unsung heroes, especially the selfless freedom fighters whose contribution to Bharat Mata had largely gone unnoticed. In the 75th year of our Independence, our book, *The Great Tribal Warriors of Bharat*, is a tribute to those uncelebrated tribal heroes who seldom made it to the history books by elite historians.

Sure enough, we have authored this book. However, without the reference material gathered from the work of scholars, history enthusiasts, authors, professors and researchers, we would not have come this far. Thanks to U Hamlet Bareh, David R. Syiemlieh, J.C. Jha, Murali Atlury, Bhangya Bhukya, S.C. Padhy, A.K. Padhy, Kalyani Pakhrin, Dr Shera Pandi Molommu, Abha Xalxo, Sita Kapadia, Arkotong Longkumer, Charu Chandra Mukherjee, Prateek Thapa of the Darjeeling Itihas Manch and Alma Grace Barla for producing substantial and authoritative work on tribal history and freedom fighters that served as the foundation for us to begin our journey.

A book like this needed a publisher who really believed in the subject. Thank you, Kapish Mehra, for your invaluable inputs and unconditional support. We are grateful to the talented team at Rupa—Yamini, Aurodeep, Sneha, Nishtha—who worked relentlessly, on a war footing, without compromising on quality to make this happen! Thank you for your suggestions. Gratitude is equally due to Anuj Bahri, proprietor of Red Ink Literary Agency,

## ACKNOWLEDGEMENTS

for facilitating the deal for this book, and to Bidisha Srivastava who worked on the initial edits.

Special thanks to Swar Khosla for designing the brilliant book cover.

For Tuhin, this book comes right after his magnum opus, *The Legend of Birsa Munda*. Tuhin would like to thank the Hon'ble Minister for Law and Justice, Shri Kiren Rijiju, for making time to write the foreword of this book. He is grateful to the Hon'ble Tribal Affairs Minister Shri Arjun Munda for graciously providing an endorsement for the book. Tuhin would equally like to thank Shri Manoj Bajpayee, Shri Mohandas Pai, Shri Amish Tripathi and Shri Aashish Chandorkar for their effusive endorsing comments for the book. Coming from such distinguished achievers, the appreciation means a lot. Tuhin would also like to thank Shri Deepak Prakash and Shri Samir Oraon, distinguished BJP leaders, who have been extremely supportive towards his previous book and shown immense enthusiasm about the content of this book.

Tuhin is grateful to Prabha Khaitan Foundation for always being so supportive in promoting quality literature. He would also like to thank his better half, Koral, and their son, Neev Tanish, for always being a pillar of support. He is immensely grateful to his vast legacy of readers built over a journey of 16 years.

A special thanks to Shri Rohit Kumar Singh, senior IAS officer, and Dr Divya Gupta, Consultant, Azadi Ka Amrit Mahotsav, Ministry of Culture, for helping us dig out some rare pictures of freedom fighters documented in this book. Even though the pictures could not be used in the book due to technical reasons, they have been extremely handy in the book promotions.

As this book comes to fruition, Ambalika would like to thank her param guru Swami Sri Yukteshwar Giri, for silently guiding her at every step, and for sending forth divine breakthroughs when her research seemed to be getting no returns. She would also like to use this opportunity to thank Nick Balmer, Mark Probett, Maya Poddar and Akhilendra Pratap Singh, whose ancestors played vital roles in various capacities during colonial times, for their generous friendship. Nick and Mark's endless appetite for scanning every possible detail about the colonial era and selflessly sharing their knowledge, so that future generations have a balanced and complete understanding of our history, has been a very important source of inspiration for Ambalika.

# BIBLIOGRAPHY

'1.9.66 | Mr. Jaipal Singh', Constitution of India, https://bit.ly/37iVSb7. Accessed on 15 April 2022.

'1996 | Live auction 5600 | Anglo-Indian', Christie's, https://bit.ly/3M3jOxN. Accessed on 14 April 2022.

'Book entitled "Footprints" by G.W. Gayer, a District Superintendent of Police in the Central Provinces', Abhilekh Patal, https://bit.ly/3Ljzj4B. Accessed on 25 March 2022.

'Constituent Assembly of India, Monday, the 5th September, 1949', Parliament of India, Lok Sabha, https://bit.ly/3qlQfz1. Accessed on 22 March 2022.

'Correspondence about dacoities committed in the Bend Provinces by Tautia Bhil and his gang', Abhilekh Patal: Portal for Access to Archives and Learning, https://bit.ly/3IThrvO. Accessed on 28 March 2022.

'Edachena Kunkan and the Siege of Panamaram Fort', Hamlet in Monsoon Blog of Ramachandran # History, Life and Polemics, https://bit.ly/3OUNdN9. Accessed on 03 May 2022.

'Freedom fighter status denied for Gobind Guru who put his life on the line for the Adivasi community', *Dainik Bhaskar*, https://bit.ly/36Cr4Sd. Accessed on 28 March 2022.

'Full text of "The Rewakantha directory"', Internet Archive, https://bit.ly/3wGeXyg. Accessed on 28 March 2022.

Gazetteer of Tahsils, Zamindaris, Towns, Important Villages, Rivers and Hills—Chandala, The Gazetteers Department, https://bit.ly/3utxRpl. Accessed on 25 March 2022.

'History', Malkangiri: Linking to the World, https://bit.ly/3wEQR72. Accessed on 28 March 2022.

'Kol Resurrection of Chota-nagpur', Internet Archive, https://bit.ly/3uuNKf3. Accessed on 25 March 2022.

'Komaram Bheem', Telangana 360, https://bit.ly/3tToh05. Accessed on 28 March 2022.

'Komaram Bheem's life ideal for tribals: Minister Satyavathi Rathod', *The Hans India*, 21 October 2021, https://bit.ly/3IN92tq. Accessed on 28 March 2022.

'Major John Henry Childe Shakespear', UBIQUE, https://bit.ly/3IDHqXG. Accessed on 25 March 2022.

'Massacre on ManGadh Hills', Desh-Daaz: Fierce Passion 4 Nation, 5 June 2013, https://bit.ly/3wGMo3G. Accessed on 28 March 2022.

'Rajasthan Distict Gazetteer of Banswara', Internet Archive, https://bit.ly/3IXSHm9. Accessed on 28 March 2022.

'Rajasthan Distict Gazetteers Dungarpur', Internet Archive, https://bit.ly/3iEogGG. Accessed on 28 March 2022.

'Recommendation of the Commissioner of Nagpore authorized Captain Shakespeare Commanding the Nagpore Irregular force', Abhilekh Patal, https://bit.ly/3tCc3IX. Accessed on 25 March 2022.

'Report on the Administration of the Dungarpur State, Rajputana For 1913-14', Internet Archive, https://bit.ly/36TIU2P. Accessed on 28 March 2022.

'Telangana committed to fulfil ideals of Komaram Bheem: KCR', *The Hans India*, 23 October 2021, https://bit.ly/3IMIFUz. Accessed on 28 March 2022.

'The First Tribal Freedom Fighter', *Telangana Today*, https://bit.ly/3Lk3qJ7. Accessed on 25 March 2022.

'The Slayer of Pazhassi Raja', Hamlet in Monsoon Blog of Ramachandran # History, Life and Polemics, https://bit.ly/3uFroZH. Accessed on 15 April 2022.

'Thomas Baber's account of the death of the Pazhassi Rajah,

Part 4', Malabar Days, https://bit.ly/3jC97pY. Accessed on 15 April 2022.

'Vocal for Local: Folklore of Vagad', DocPlayer, https://bit.ly/3uHzaSZ. Accessed on 14 April 2022.

'Veer Baburao Shedmake: A Tribal Revolutionary', *Hello Maharashtra*, 21 October 2021, https://bit.ly/3uomFKC. Accessed on 25 March 2022.

Arnold, David, 'Sitarama Raju's Rebellion: A Response', *Social Scientist*, Vol. 13, No. 4, 1985, pp. 44-49.

Arora, Sakshi, 'This tribal leader who opposed prohibition also led India to first Olympic hockey gold', *The Print*, 14 August 2018, https://bit.ly/3ufwkmE. Accessed on 22 March 2022.

Atlury, Murali, 'Alluri Sitarama Raju and the Manyam Rebellion of 1922-1924', *Social Scientist*, Vol. 12, No. 4, 1984, pp. 3-33.

Bareh, Hamlet, *U Tirot Singh*, Publications Division Ministry of Information & Broadcasting, 2017.

Barla, Alma Grace, *Indigenous Heroines: A Saga of Tribal Women of India*, IWGIA, 2015.

Behuria, N.C., *Final Report on the Major Settlement Operations in Koraput District 1938-64*, Orissa Govt Press, Cuttack, 1966.

Bhagat, Amit, 'Baburao Shedmake: Adivasi Hero of 1857', Live History India, 9 May 2019, https://bit.ly/3LcKvQn. Accessed on 25 March 2022.

Bhukya, Bhangya, 'Between Tradition and Modernity: Nizams, Colonialism and Modernity in Hyderabad State', *Economic and Political Weekly*, Vol. 48, No. 48, 2013, pp. 120-125.

Bhukya, Bhangya, 'The Subordination of the Sovereigns: Colonialism and the Gond Rajas in Central India, 1818-1948', *Modern Asian Studies*, Vol. 47, No. 1, 2013, pp. 288-317.

Biswas, A.K., 'Jaipal Singh Munda: Hockey champion and the voice of the voiceless', *Forward Press*, 8 April 2018, https://bit.ly/3uKz4Kr. Accessed on 15 April 2022.

Chattoraj, A.K., 'The Tana Bhagat Movement: An Appraisal',

*Proceedings of the Indian History Congress,* Vol. 60, 1999, pp. 639-644.

Dasgupta, Sangeeta, 'Reading Adivasi Histories: Tana Bhagats in Colonial and Postcolonial Times', *Colloquium 2012-2013: "Hinterlands, Frontiers, Cities, and States: Transactions and Identities",* Yale Macmillian Center: Program in Agrarian Studies, https://bit.ly/3Daw3pc. Accessed on 25 March 2022.

Desai, I.P., 'The Vedchhi Movement (A Sociological Essay)', Centre for Regional Development Studies, Surat, https://bit.ly/36NmTD2. Accessed on 25 March 2022.

*Dictionary of Martyrs: India's Freedom Struggle (1857-1947), Vol. 5,* Ministry of Culture, Government of India and Indian Council of Historical Research, 2018.

Faruqui, Munis D., 'At Empire's End: The Nizam, Hyderabad and Eighteenth-Century India', *Modern Asian Studies,* Vol. 43, No. 1, 2009, pp. 5-43.

Fischer-Tine, Harald, Michael Mann. *Colonialism as Civilizing Mission: Cultural Ideology in British India,* Anthem Press, 2004.

Fuchs, Stephen, 'Messianic Movements in Primitive India', *Asian Folklore Studies,* Vol. 24, No. 1, 1965, pp. 11-62.

Gott, Richard, *Britain's Empire: Resistance, Repression and Revolt,* Verso Books, 2011.

Grant, Charles, *The Gazetteer of the Central Provinces of India,* Education Society's Press Chief, 1867.

Hunter, William Wilson, *Annals of Rural Bengal,* Smith, Elder and Company, United Kingdom, 1871.

Hunter, William Wilson, *The Imperial Gazetteer of India,* Volume 12, Trübner & Company, London, 1887.

Idlet, John Thomas, *Evangelising the Nation: Religion and the Formation of Naga Political Identity,* Routledge, 2015.

Jackson, Will, Emily Manktelow, *Subverting Empire: Deviance and Disorder in the British Colonial World,* Springer, 2015.

Jha, Amar Nath, 'Locating the Ancient History of Santal

Parganas', *Proceedings of the Indian History Congress*, Vol. 70, 2009-2010, pp. 185-196.

Jha, J.C., 'The Kol Rising of Chotanagpur (1831-33)—Its Causes', *Proceedings of the Indian History Congress*, Vol. 21, 1958, pp. 440-446.

Jha, J.C., 'A Sad Episode of the Kol Insurrection (1832)', *Proceedings of the Indian History Congress*, Vol. 42, 1981, pp. 413-418.

Jha, J.D., 'Nature of the Kol Insurrection of 1831-32', *Proceedings of the Indian History Congress*, Vol. 24, 1961, pp. 217-222.

Johari, Shubha, 'Annexation of Nagpur', *Proceedings of the Indian History Congress*, Vol. 68/Part One, 2007, pp. 547-552.

Kapadia, Sita, 'Windfall: Tribal Women Come Through', *Women's Studies Quarterly*, Vol. 17, No. 3/4, 1989, pp. 140-149.

Kumar, Anil, 'An Unknown Chapter of Kol-Insurrection', *Proceedings of the Indian History Congress*, Vol. 62, 2001, pp. 621-626.

Kumar, Sanjay, 'The Tana Bhagat Movement in Chotanagpur (1914-1920)', *Proceedings of the Indian History Congress*, Vol. 69, 2008, pp. 723-731.

Longkumer, Arkotong, 'Religious and Economic Reform: The Gaidinliu Movement and the Heraka in the North Cachar Hills', *Journal of South Asian Studies*, Vol. 30, No. 3, 2007, pp. 499 -515, DOI:10.1080/00856400701714096.

Longkumer, Arkotong, "Cleanliness is next to godliness": Religious change, hygiene and the renewal of Heraka villages in Assam', *Contributions to Indian Sociology*, Vol. 45, No. 2, 2011, pp. 189 -216, DOI:10.1177/006996671104500202.

Longkumer, Arkotong, "Lines that speak": The Gaidinliu notebooks as language, prophecy, and textuality', *Journal of Ethnographic Theory*, Vol. 6, No. 2, 2016, pp. 123 -147, DOI:10.14318/hau6.2.011.

Mahadevan, Raman, 'Zeliangrong Naga Uprising Of 1930-32: A Brief Summary', *Proceedings of the Indian History Congress*, Vol. 35, 1974, pp. 253-259.

Mahurkar, Uday, 'The Massacre on Mangadh Hill: The Biggest Sacrifice Buried in History', *Aaj Tak*, 4 September 2012, https://bit.ly/3Nl4yxX. Accessed on 28 March 2022.

Mahurkar, Uday, 'Descendants of Mangad massacre seek recognition for past tragedy', *India Today*, 10 September 2012, https://bit.ly/3uCANjH. Accessed on 28 March 2022.

Mangamma, J., 'Gudem Rebellion of 1922—Forest Administration as a Cause', *Proceedings of the Indian History Congress*, Vol. 40, 1979, pp. 628–635.

Mehta, Shirin M., 'The Bardoli satyagraha of 1928: A Note on Organizations', *Proceedings of the Indian History Congress*, Vol. 39, No. II, 1978, pp. 597–605.

Mishra, P.L., 'The Annexation of the Nagpur State', *Proceedings of the Indian History Congress*, Vol. 30, 1968, pp. 259–267.

Molommu, Shera Pandi, 'Helen Lepcha Alias Sabitri Devi: Lone Freedom Fighter From the Lepcha Tribe', *International Journal of Informative & Futuristic Research*, Vol. 2, No. 9, 2015, pp. 3242 -3246, https://bit.ly/3Dbx1BJ. Accessed on 25 March 2022.

Molommu, Shera Pandi, 'Dal Bahadur Giri—The First Gorkha Freedom Fighter from Darjeeling Hills', *Research Guru: Online Journal of Multidisciplinary Studies*, Vol. 11, No. 4, 2018, pp. 106–116. Mukherjee, Charu Chandra, *The Life of Tantia Bhil: The renowned bandit-chief,* B.H. Dutt, Calcutta, 1890.

Nair, Gopalan, C. *Wynad, Its Peoples and Traditions*, Asian Educational Services, 2000.

Nath, Sanjay, 'Remembering Poto Ho: The Leader of Adivasi Anti-British Resistance in Kolhan (1836-37)' *Journal of Adivasi and Indigenous Studies*, Vol. 9, No. 1, 2019), pp. 1–25.

Nayak, Birendra, 'Hanging of Laxman Naik: A Tribal Gandhite', *The Tribal Tribune*, https://bit.ly/3NroLSv. Accessed on 28 March 2022.

Nilsen, Alf Gunvald, 'Subalterns and the State in the Longue Durée: Notes from "The Rebellious Century" in the Bhil

Heartland', *Journal of Contemporary Asia*, Vol. 45, No. 4, 2015, pp. 574–595, https://bit.ly/3vgbNyQ. Accessed on 14 April 2022.

Niumai, Ajailiu, 'Rani Gaidinliu: The Iconic Woman of Northeast India', *Indian Journal of Gender Studies*, Vol. 25, No. 3, 2018, pp. 351–367, DOI:10.1177/0971521518785666.

Padhy, S.C., A.K. Padhy and S.C. Pathy, 'Lakshman Naik Tribal Freedom Fighter and Martyr', *Proceedings of the Indian History Congress*, Vol. 59, 1998, pp. 587–594.

Pakhrin, Kalyani, 'Challenging the Hegemons: The Unheard Story of a Brave Woman, Putalimaya Devi Poddar', *IOSR Journal of Humanities and Social Science (IOSR-JHSS)* Vol. 10, No. 2, 2013, pp. 53–60.

Pati, Biswamoy, 'Storm Over Malkangiri: A Preliminary Note on Laxman Naiko's Revolt (1942)', *Proceedings of the Indian History Congress*, Vol. 41, 1980, pp. 706–721.

Pezarkar, Leora, 'The Mangarh Massacre', Live History India, 6 August 2017, https://bit.ly/37VNDBE. Accessed on 28 March 2022.

Kumar, Ramnaresh, 'Komaram Bheem—The man who led the tribal revolt against Hyderabad's Nizam', Dakshināvarta,, 29 October 2020, https://bit.ly/3JPJrBt. Accessed on 28 March 2022

Prasad, Archana, 'Military Conflict and Forests in Central Provinces, India: Gonds and the Gondwana Region in Pre-colonial History', *Environment and History*, Vol. 5, No. 3, 1999, pp. 361–375.

Priyadarshi, Ashok, 'Tribal Rebellions in North Orissa: A Study On Kol Uprising Of Mayurbhanj State (1821–1836)', *Proceedings of the Indian History Congress*, Vol. 71, 2010–2011, pp. 696–705.

Ramachandran, D.P., *Empire's First Soldiers*, Lancer Publishers, 2008.

Rao, Trinadha Palla, 'Telangana State land survey should uphold rights of tribals', Land Portal, 7 September 2017, https://bit.ly/3NsD0GV. Accessed on 28 March 2022.

Sane, Hemant, 'Nagpur and Mutiny of 1857', Academia, https://bit.ly/36S5rNO. Accessed on 25 March 2022.

Sharma, Jyotirmaya, 'This Girl is Very Dangerous', Debating India, 10 April 2005, https://bit.ly/3Ntp5Ag. Accessed on 28 March 2022.

Shedmake, Shatali, 'The Life Story of the Adivasi Revolutionary of Chandrapur "Baburao Pullesur Shedmake"', *Adivasi Resurgence*, 12 February 2018, https://bit.ly/3JIkvfc. Accessed on 25 March 2022.

Sharma, Suryamani (Ed.), *Hamra Swantantrata Senani*, Sumeru Publication, Siliguri, 1990, p. 76.

Singh, Harpal S., 'Babejhari merits its place in history', *The Hindu*, 27 October 2015, https://bit.ly/3JS1Rle. Accessed on 28 March 2022.

Singh, Harpal S., 'Titles have disrupted rights of tribals on forest land', *The Hindu*, 2 July 2019, https://bit.ly/3wGfzny. Accessed on 28 March 2022.

Singh, Hitler, 'In the den of Rani Gaidinliu the legendary freedom fighter—Mount Kisha at Magulong Village', E-Pao, https://bit.ly/3xrwkTH. Accessed on 14 April 2022.

Sinha, B.K.P., 'Deforestation in India during British rule', *Daily Pioneer*, 22 September 2021, https://bit.ly/36v1X3Z. Accessed on 28 March 2022.

Syiemlieh, David R., 'In Pursuit of History: Discussion on the Collection and Interpretation of Data Introduction', *The NEHU Journal*, Vol. XIII, No. 2, 2015, pp. 1–15.

*The Calcutta Review, Volume 36*, Calcutta University Press, 1861.

Equitable Tourism Options, *This is Our Homeland: A Collection of Essays on the Betrayal of Adivasi Rights in India*, Equations, 2007.

Vashistha, Vijay Kumar, 'The Bhil Revolt Of 1913 under Guru Govindgiri Among the Bhils of Southern Rajasthan and its

Impact', *Proceedings of the Indian History Congress*, Vol. 52, 1991, pp. 522–527.

von Fürer-Haimendorf, Christoph, *Tribes of India the Struggle for Survival*, University of California Press, Berkeley, 1 July 1992, p. 360.

von Fürer-Haimendorf, Christoph, von Fürer-Haimendorf, Elizabeth, *The Gonds of Andhra Pradesh: Tradition and Change in an Indian Tribe*, Routledge, 1979.

Watson, Archibald, *Memoir of the Late David Scott*, Baptist Mission Press, 1832.

Wellesley, Arthur, *Supplementary Despatches and Memoranda of Field Marshal Arthur Duke of Wellington*, K.G., John Murray, London, 1859.

William, Logan, 'Malabar Manual, Vol. 1', Internet Archive, https://bit.ly/3vWfiuE. Accessed on 02 May 2022.

Xalxo, Abha, 'The Great Santal Insurrection (Hul) of 1855-56', *Proceedings of the Indian History Congress*, Vol. 69, 2008, pp. 732–755.

# INDEX

1857 war of independence, xiv

Adivasi, xii, xiv, 2, 83, 116, 117, 118, 119, 120, 122, 123, 124, 136, 137, 143
Ambedkar, B.R., Dr, xi, xv, 123
Azadi ka Amrit Mahotsav, xii

Bhagat, Budhu, xiv, 18, 21, 24
Bhagat Movement, xv, 69, 74, 75, 79
Bhairab, 38, 40, 41, 42, 43, 45, 46
Bharatiya Janata Party, 83, 134, 135, 151
Bheem, Komaram, xv, 57, 102, 103, 108
Bhil, xiv, xv, 58, 59, 60, 62, 65, 66, 67, 68, 69, 71, 72, 73, 74, 75
Bhil, Tantya, xiv, 58
Bonda, 93
Bose, Subhas Chandra, xi, 110

Chand, 38, 40, 41, 42, 43, 44, 46
Chanda, 48, 49, 50, 51, 53, 55
Chanthu, Thalakkal, xiv, 8, 9, 11
charkha, 82, 97, 112, 147
Chaudhury, Dashriben, xiv, 136
Chauri Chaura incident, 92
Chota Nagpur, 21, 22, 24, 77, 78, 79, 81, 120
Chota Nagpur Tenancy Act, 78
civil disobedience movement, 98
colonial biases, xii
colonialism, 86
Congress, 22, 38, 72, 75, 79, 82, 83, 86, 92, 93, 94, 95, 96, 97, 98, 99, 101, 110, 111, 112, 113, 114, 115, 119, 144, 146, 147, 148, 149
Constituent Assembly, xiv, 116, 117, 119, 120, 121, 123, 124
Constitution, 116, 121, 122, 124
conversion, xiii, 56, 133
Criminal Tribes Act, 116

dacoit, 22, 60
Dalit, 123
Damin-i-Koh, 5, 39, 40, 43, 47
Devi, Sabitri, 109, 110, 112, 113, 114, 115, 145
drinking, 70, 75, 107, 137, 138

Fifth Schedule, 120, 121, 122
First World War, 77, 111, 133, 138
Fituri, 87, 88, 90, 91, 96
forests, 10, 17, 49, 56, 57, 91, 102, 103, 104
freedom fighters, xiii, xiv, xv, 83, 100, 114, 115, 150
freedom struggle, xi, xii, 47, 66, 92, 111, 112, 114, 139, 143, 145, 146, 149

Gaidinliu, Rani, xiv, 125, 127, 128, 129, 134
Giri, Gobind, Guru, xv, 66, 67, 68, 71
Gond, xiv, xv, 48, 49, 50, 51, 52, 53, 54, 55, 56, 57, 102, 103, 104, 105, 106, 107, 108
Gond, Ramji, 48, 53, 55, 56, 104, 105
Gorkha, 114, 144
guerrilla warfare, 1, 5, 13, 22, 31, 64, 107, 116

*hul*, 7, 41, 42, 43, 46

independence, 51, 87, 89, 92, 100, 112, 132, 146

Indian Forest Act, 138

Kaliparaj, 136, 138, 139
Kanhu, xiv, 38, 40, 41, 43, 44, 45, 46
Khasi, xiv, 26, 27, 28, 29, 30, 31, 35, 36, 37
Khilafat Movement, xii
Kol, xiv, 18, 19, 21, 22, 23, 24
Koya, 84, 88, 90, 91, 96
Kunkan, Edachena, 9
Kurichiyan, xiv, 8, 9, 11, 12, 13, 14, 16, 17

Land Acquisition Act, 138
Larka, 20, 21, 24
Lepcha, Helen, xiv, 109, 110, 111, 115, 145

Madras Estates Land Act, 95
Mahajan, 38, 39, 40, 41, 43, 44
Mahatma Gandhi, xiv, 86, 92, 94, 112, 136, 137, 139, 142, 147
Manjhi, 4, 39, 40, 47
Manjhi, Tilka, xiii, 1, 2, 3, 4, 5, 6, 7, 124
Modi, Narendra, PM, xii, 150
Munda, xii, xiv, xv, 7, 47, 116, 117, 118, 119, 120, 121, 122, 124, 151
Munda, Birsa, xii, xv, 47, 151
Munda, Jaipal Singh, 116, 118
muttadar, 85, 87, 90, 91
Muttadar, 88

Nath Panthi, 66

# INDEX

Nayak, Laxman, xiv, 93
Nepali, 144, 145, 148
Nizam of Hyderabad, 49, 56, 102, 104
non-cooperation movement, 81
Nongkhlaw, 26, 27, 28, 29, 30, 31, 32, 34, 36, 37

Oraon, xiv, 25, 77, 78, 79, 80, 81, 83, 151
Oraon, Jatra, xiv, 77, 83

Paharia, 5
Patel, Vallabhbhai, Sardar, xi
Permanent Settlement Act, 40
prohibition, 97, 122, 123

Quit India, 93, 98, 101, 143, 144, 148

Raju, Sitarama, Alluri, xiv, 84, 88, 96
revolt, xiii, xiv, 17, 21, 23, 51, 52, 53, 56, 75, 96, 97, 103, 131

Santhal, xiv, 2, 6, 7, 38, 40, 41, 44, 45, 46, 47, 123
satyagraha, 98, 99, 112, 137
Seditious Meetings Act, 82
Shedmake, Baburao, xiv, 48, 51, 104, 105
shifting cultivation, 80, 84, 95, 130
Sidhu, xiv, 38, 40, 41, 42, 43, 44, 45

Sing, Tirot, U, xiv, 26, 27, 36, 37
Sonthal Parganas Act, 46
subaltern, xi, xii, 119, 124
Swadeshi movement, 86, 110
Syiem, 27, 28, 29, 30, 31, 33, 34, 35, 36, 37

Tamang, Putalimaya, Devi, 144
Tana Bhagat, 78, 79, 80, 81, 82, 83
tax, 3, 4, 10, 11, 12, 20, 24, 40, 70, 95, 103, 131, 136
the British, xiii, xiv, 2, 3, 4, 5, 6, 9, 10, 12, 13, 17, 19, 21, 22, 23, 26, 27, 30, 31, 32, 33, 34, 35, 36, 37, 39, 40, 42, 44, 46, 50, 51, 52, 55, 56, 62, 66, 67, 70, 71, 73, 74, 75, 76, 77, 78, 79, 80, 82, 83, 84, 85, 86, 87, 88, 90, 91, 92, 93, 95, 96, 98, 101, 104, 112, 113, 114, 116, 121, 125, 126, 127, 128, 130, 131, 132, 133, 137, 138, 144, 145, 146, 147
the Northeast, xiv, 32
tribal, xiii, xiv, xv, 20, 24, 25, 45, 85, 87, 98, 103, 110, 116, 117, 119, 122, 123, 143, 150

Varma, Kerala, Pazhassi Raja, xiv, 8, 10
Vedar, 8

zamindar, 5, 20, 25, 39, 40, 41, 42, 44, 45, 49, 50, 51, 52, 53,

59, 60, 61, 62, 65, 68, 77, 78,
80, 97, 98, 102, 103, 104, 105

Zeliangrong, 125, 127, 128, 129,
130, 133, 134